DUCK PLUCKER

A father and son's funny, crazy, short stories from the farm about raising cattle, horses, hunting, neighbors, friends, and a lifetime of adventures in rural Ohio.

Ted Martin, Jr.

 Ted Martin Publishing.

ISBN-13: 978-0615922744

ISBN-10: 0615922740

Visit Amazon.com to order additional copies.

Dedicated to my father:

Dr. Theodore B. Martin, a/k/a "Doc."

Thanks for everything, Doc, you're one of a kind!

Theodore B. Martin, Jr.

Devoted Son and Raconteur

Prologue

I was raised in Middletown, Ohio, between Dayton and Cincinnati. Our farm, Martin Meadows, was off Route 4 between Middletown and Hamilton. Doc's grandpa started with dairy cattle, but his father switched to Black Angus so he could work at Armco Steel as a foreman. Doc stuck with Black Angus. We had seventy-five head, plus every other farm animal that existed. My father, Ted "Doc" Martin, was the first Martin to go to college; all his relatives were farmers in the area.

He became the first orthodontist in Middletown, so our cows had the straightest teeth in Butler County.

Ted Martin, Jr.

DUCK PLUCKER

Ted Martin, Jr.

Table of Contents

"Doc" Martin's Farm Vocabulary

Doc has his own vocabulary. He has so many unique personal sayings that you need a guidebook to interpret what he meant: If someone was constipated, they were "egg-locked."

If their back was out, they were "stoved up."

If they had an upset stomach, they had a "blotation."

If they were nauseous and not hungry, they were "loggy."

A "cock-block" was any general malaise that prevented you from doing what you wanted to do.

If you asked Doc how he felt, he might put all the above together, and answer with, "Well, I'm egg-locked with a bad blotation, plus I'm feelin' loggy from being all stoved up; someone must have put a cock-block on me."

"What the Sam Hell are you doing?" "What the hell's going on?" "All hell's breaking loose!" and "Keeerighsssttt!!!" – All meant the same thing, chaos.

"Like a Bat out of Hell." – Meant moving very fast.

"Hog Waller" – Hog manure, mud, and slop all combined in a low piece of land to create a nasty bog for the hogs to lie in.

"Duck Plucker" – A farmers' homemade contraption for plucking feathers off a dead duck.

“Blown to Smithereens” or “Kablooey.” – What happened to the fence after the cow or horse went through it.

“Coming in Hot” – Fast approaching on a horse and not able to stop in time to avoid hitting something or someone.

“Hog wash” – Stands for BS.

“Make it easy on yourself.” – Means Doc believed he has the upper hand, as in, asking him how much he wants to bet on something, his reply of “Make it easy on yourself” means bet as much as you want because you are going to lose the bet.

Eaton Cattle Auction

We raised Black Angus cattle on the Martin Meadows farm, and the Eaton Cattle Auction was our nearest market. Eaton is about an hour away, via very hilly back country roads. We used an old horse trailer to transport cows we were buying and selling, and we usually bought and sold on the same trip.

Doc had a cattle adviser; call him Rob Poolman, who supposedly knew a lot about building a Black Angus herd. Poolman would show up at our farm the day we were heading out and look over our herd, then advise us on what we needed to buy that day at the auction to make the herd better. Then he would ride with us over to Eaton. Poolman was an alcoholic with a stuttering problem. He would drink all the way over to Eaton, even if we were leaving at 9:00 a.m. Then he and Doc would walk around the stalls and review all the cattle to be auctioned that day. Doc would make notes and establish a rank order of what they would bid on. Poolman would be the expert on what would be the maximum price we would pay for each one, as well as reserving the right to change his mind based on price/value correlations in the auction process. Then we would sit in the stands with the rest of the buyers, waiting for each bull, cow, steer, or calf to be auctioned off.

The problem was that Poolman was always completely bombed by the time the auction started, right after lunch. All the notes and preparation would fly out the window as soon as the first cow was introduced to the ring. Poolman would get excited and start stuttering, " Th-th-th-th-th," and the auctioneer would hear him stutter, and take it as a bid. Doc would turn to him and say, "What the Sam Hell are you doing?" and Poolman would stutter some more, "The-the-the-th," which would cause another bid. Next thing you know, Doc had bought the cow. Once Poolman had settled down, he would finally say, "The-the-the-that's the one we decided not to buy." And Doc would check his notes and see it was one they had decided in the walk-around that morning not to bid on, at any price. So the entire auction would turn into chaos for Doc, because his advisor was too deep into the sauce and he stuttered. But we would end up with some cows and calves and maybe a new young bull and head back toward our farm with a heavy load of hoof in the horse trailer.

The horse trailer looked like it was going to break down even with nothing in it, and with two thousand pounds of Black Angus, it really looked like it was going to blow apart.

And that is exactly what it did on the way home one Saturday afternoon. The rear axle on the trailer snaps, and we go careening off into a ditch. Now we have a broken trailer in the ditch with a cow and calf, and we need to get back to our farm to fetch another trailer to get these animals home. Of course, our back-up trailer is in worse shape than the trailer that just broke, but that's beside the point. We wait by the side of the road, and after an hour, someone must have called the sheriff. The sheriff shows up and starts examining the situation. After walking around the trailer, he asks Doc for his driver's license. Doc does not have his driver's license with him, he explains, as he left it on his dresser. The reality is that his license was revoked in the state of Ohio many years ago.

"Let's see the car registration," the sheriff says.

No car registration or insurance card in the glove box of the pickup. Just lots of pliers, staples, wire, shotgun shells, and a flask. The sheriff checks the license plate on the pickup, and finds it to be several years out of date.

He now lists the issues. "You have no driver's license, the pickup has an expired license plate, you have no registration, and no insurance card. The trailer has expired plates, and no brake light hook-up. What do you think you are doing?"

Doc explains that the pickup only left the farm once a year, as did the trailer, to go back and forth to the Eaton Cattle Auction. We had never had a problem before, because we never wrecked before.

The sheriff says, "Well, you got a problem now."

Doc explains that we need a ride back to our farm to get the other trailer.

"You are not going anywhere except the courthouse, since you are driving without a license."

The sheriff gets two tow trucks, one truck to tow our busted trailer, and the other to tow our pickup truck to the courthouse in Eaton. We call my mom. She drives over and posts bail for Doc and we drive home. The poor cow and calf are still in the broken trailer in the parking lot of the Eaton sheriff's station. We wait until it gets dark and late, and then we drive the replacement trailer over to Eaton and park next to the broken trailer. At midnight, we successfully move the cow and calf from one trailer to the other. We use the spare keys to get into the pickup truck, and we each drive home.

The broken trailer is worthless, so we plan on just leaving it. The court date arrives and Doc is in front of the judge, pleading his case. The first question the judge asks is, "How did you get here?"

Doc quickly says that his wife drove him over and dropped him off, and she has gone shopping. He is not a good liar, and the judge is slightly amused that he has taken this kind of risk, with all the violations already listed.

The judge says, "Are you the orthodontist over in Middletown?"

Doc answers, "Why yes, I am."

"You did a great job on my daughter's teeth," says the judge. The judge likes Doc and lets him off with a $100 fine and life moves on.

A month later, we are driving together on I-75, heading to Cincinnati, when a sheriff pulls out from hiding and signals us to pull over.

The officer comes up to my dad's window and says, "You were speeding," to which Doc quickly replies, "I was just keeping up with the cars in front of me."

The sheriff says, "You ever hunt ducks?" and Doc replies, "Sure I hunt ducks, you want to come over for some great duck hunting at our farm pond?" and the sheriff says, "No thanks, but let me ask you something. When you hunt ducks, do you shoot at the whole flock or at one duck?"

To which Doc replies, "I shoot at one duck."

And the sheriff says, "Exactly. And today, you are the duck!"

The UPS Truck

The problem with buying cows at the Eaton Cattle Auction is that the cows have an innate built-in homing device. They know that in the morning, they lived on one farm, the farm where all their cow buddies still live and the farm they consider home. Now it is late afternoon and they have been sold and bought at a cattle auction, then transported to a new farm where they don't know any of the cows and nothing is familiar. So naturally they want to go home, and they have a pretty good sense in which direction lies their home farm. As soon as it gets dark, they start heading in that direction, and the fences better be strong because they are going to try and go back to the farm they know. They tend to wait until night to make their move, probably because they cannot get to sleep in the unfamiliar surroundings.

Our farm sits back a half mile east of a rural highway Route 4. The highway runs between Middletown and Hamilton. We have never bought a cow from east of our farm. All the cows we have ever purchased from the Eaton Cattle Auction are from west of our farm, so the cows all head west when they try and leave our farm, which means they must cross Route 4 as they try to head home after escaping.

We had just purchased a cow and calf combination, our favorite and most common "buy" at the Eaton Cattle Auction. It's 2:00 a.m. and the phone rings that night in the farmhouse.

It's the sheriff, informing us that a UPS truck had struck one of our cows out on the highway.

Doc woke me up and said, "Get dressed, we have one down out on Route 4." We immediately assume what had transpired. The cow and calf had broken through our fence to head home, and a UPS truck had struck the cow as it attempted to cross Route 4. We jump into the pickup and get out there to see the sheriff's car blocking any cars that might come along from the southbound lanes, flashers on. A UPS truck is flipped over on its side after hitting the cow, and is lying across the southbound lanes. The cow is also in the middle of the lanes in a sitting position. The cow is very much alive but has been hit badly, her back end blown wide open by the impact. While the cow is in the "sitting" position, it needs to be put out of its misery. We did not bring a gun with us, since we assumed the cow was dead when we got the phone call. The calf has not been hit and is standing nearby on the side of the road; we could round him up later. The driver of the UPS truck is shaken up but not injured, and he is standing by the side of the road as well. He was protected by his seatbelt in the crash.

"I never saw it until I hit it," he says, "then I swerved from the impact and flipped the truck."

My dad walks up to the sheriff and says, "You need to shoot the cow in the head and put her out of her misery."

The sheriff is a large man, 6'4", 250 pounds, African American, and he is a "command and control" type of sheriff, as most were back then. The sheriff says, "What we have here is a situation," as he clearly is unsure what to do.

Doc says, "You need to put the cow out of its misery."

Sheriff says, "I will tell you what to do, you don't tell me what to do."

Doc replies, "Fine, hand me your gun and tell me to put the cow down."

The sheriff says, "I will put the cow down." Mr. Tough Sheriff is clearly in over his head at how and where to shoot the cow. The sheriff pulls out his .45 pistol and approaches the head of the cow. He levels his aim at the head, but he flinches badly as he closes his eyes and jerks the trigger. The bullet misses the cow's head completely, ricochets off the highway pavement, and shatters the windshield of the UPS truck next to the cow. The driver jumps and backs off the shoulder of the highway and the calf runs off.

We look on in disbelief as Doc deadpans, "You missed."

The sheriff levels his gun at the cow's head again; this time, his whole arm shakes. He closes his eyes again as he pulls the trigger, and the bullet glances off the forehead of the cow, causing a river of blood to flow down the cow's face. The cow is not dead or unconscious, and she now lets loose the loudest bawl I have ever heard from a cow before, while blood runs down her face.

The sheriff faints and falls over backward, striking his head on the highway. A pool of blood forms behind his head and he is out, stone cold unconscious.

Doc walks over to the sheriff and takes the .45, which is lying next to the sheriff on the highway. He then walks over to the cow and shoots it in the side of the head, immediately killing the cow. The UPS driver is no longer within sight.

It's a hot summer night and the windows are rolled down in the sheriff's car. Doc tells me to get on the sheriff's radio and call for help as he tries to stop the bleeding on the back of the sheriff's head, who is still unconscious.

I open the sheriff's driver door, hop in, and key the mic and say, "We need help!"

The dispatcher immediately responds and asks, "Any shots fired, anyone down?"

I quickly count the shots and report, "Three shots fired, one sheriff down," and the dispatch quickly replies, "Stand by for back-up!"

I get out of the patrol car and say to Doc, "They're sending back-up."

"Back-up," he says, "does that mean an ambulance?"

"Not sure," I say.

Ten minutes later, a state highway patrol car comes flying down Route 4 toward us. There are no lights on Route 4, and the UPS truck is flipped on its side with no lights on. The back-up sheriff is "coming in hot," because back-up is required. The unconscious sheriff's patrol car with the lights flashing is on the other side of the UPS truck. The approaching sheriff has no idea there is an "invisible" brown UPS truck lying on its side blocking the road. The sheriff sees the brown UPS truck in his headlights when it is too late; he slams on his brakes, and swerves sideways into the back of the UPS truck. He destroys the side of his patrol car and the back end of the UPS truck.

The UPS driver, who had come back to the side of his UPS truck, once again retreats into the woods. Doc and I look at each other, realizing we should have taken the flashlight from the unconscious officer to try and warn any traffic coming from the other direction.

The second sheriff is in disbelief at what just happened. He calls for an ambulance and two tow trucks. The ambulance crew arrives, revives the sheriff, and they take him away for stitches and to check for a concussion. A wrecker pushes the damaged UPS truck to the side of the road. We then help the tow truck drag the dead cow to the side of the road. We find the calf a little later and get him back onto our farm, and it's 3:00 a.m. before we get back in bed.

The Knobby Whacker

The next day we worked on getting rid of thc damaged dead cow. Because we own it, we have to dispose of it. That means a trip to Charlie the Knobby Whacker, a/k/a the local meat processor. We called him the Knobby Whacker because he cut the cow up along the knobs (the joints) before cutting the meat away from the bones. We are able to use the forklift to get two pallets underneath the cow and secure them around the cow with a rope. We then hook up a chain to the cow's neck and attach that to the back of the tractor. The cow is dragging about twenty feet behind the tractor as we set off down Route 4, towing the cow on skids. We need to make it just two miles to the turn-off, but we are in trouble right off the bat. The cow was pretty damaged from the hit by the UPS truck. A hind leg that was hanging off the pallet detached after a half a mile, looking like road kill on the side of the highway.

"We just lost a leg!" I yelled as Doc turned up the throttle on the tractor. The rule with the Knobby Whacker is that you have to get the cow there for processing within twenty-four hours of death or the Knobby Whacker won't take it. A hundred yards later, we lose another piece of hindquarters, followed by a stomach. We are losing pieces of cow every hundred yards, and then the back pallet splinters into pieces and we start dropping more parts of cow on the highway. By the time we make it to the Knobby Whacker, we deliver a head attached to a neck; the rest of the cow is strewn all over Route 4.

"At least we can process the tongue," quips Doc in his typical humorous fashion.

One winter, a cow wandered onto our frozen pond and crashed through the ice. The cow tried to get to shore but it was stuck in the ice. Its head was sticking out above the ice and the pond froze over the next day around the cow's frozen dead head. It was a very strange sight to see a frozen cow head on top of the pond all winter. We put a chain around the frozen head and tied it to a tree onshore and waited for spring. As soon as the first thaw occurred in early spring, we dragged her up onto land with the tractor. Since she was still frozen, we decided to head right onto the highway and use the frozen carcass as a buffer to the asphalt, no pallets needed. We got to the Knobby Whacker with cow intact, and the frozen carcass slid nicely down the highway with low friction. It slid almost too nicely. The cow fishtailed all over the highway and would not stay behind the tractor in our lane.

"How long has she been dead?" asked Mr. Knobby Whacker.

"Just yesterday; she fell in, drowned, and froze," said Doc.

The Knobby Whacker processed the cow for us, and a week later, we showed up to pick up the meat. We cooked a steak, and it was unbelievably good! We had accidentally just invented a technique later known as "Supercooling," and from then on we lured one cow a year out onto the semi-frozen ice with hay in the middle of the icy pond. Supercooling swept the beef processing industry and is still used today to create the most tender steaks. Unfortunately, we failed to patent the technique.

We had a livestock scale on the farm, so Doc knew how much each cow weighed before we got to the Knobby Whacker. That way he knew if he was being cheated, plus, he would bet Charlie on who could guess the weight the closest. We would show up with something dead, and Charlie prided himself on guessing within ten pounds on an animal that could weigh up to 1,000 pounds. But Doc already knew the exact weight, and Charlie did not know we had a scale.

"Bet you five dollars on who gets closer," Doc would say.

Charlie would look the animal over, and say nine hundred fifty pounds. And Doc would say nine hundred fifty-five. Then the animal would weigh in at nine hundred fifty-seven pounds. Doc knew not to guess the exact weight, or the gig would be up; plus, each scale is a bit different, anyway. Charlie never figured out that Doc had a scale on his farm. The one time Charlie visited our farm to look for a scale, Doc covered it with hay bales.

Roundups

A "roundup" at the farm is when you decide you need to bring the whole herd up to the barn and corral them. It gives you a chance to ear-tag any cows that need it, castrate young bulls, remove coke-bottle flies (blow flies) from the backs of the Black Angus, spray fly repellant on their faces, etc. In general, it is a chance to check the whole herd and take care of them, checking for disease, injuries, and tagging. We used BB guns to roundup the herd, as a shot to the flank would sting the cow but never penetrate the hide. Doc always inevitably needed to shoot one of my sisters with a BB to the butt. It really stung through blue jeans. He shot me once and I simply turned and quickly shot him back. From then on we had a truce. But he always had to shoot someone in the fanny with a BB gun. It was in his nature and you could not take it out of him.

We invited friends to come out and help with roundups, and Doc always had to trick someone into touching the electric fence, as well. He would take a small dry stick and touch the fence, and say, "see, it's off." Then he would tell the other person to check it, and they would pick a stick that still had some "green" to it, and the moisture in the stick would conduct the charge and shock the person. Or he would tell them to use a blade of grass, and that always carried the current as well. Same with the 8-battery cattle prod. He would always find a way to "accidentally" bump someone with it or talk them into testing it out on themselves. Of course, we laughed very hard when the victim jumped and yelled from touching one of the electric fences or the cattle prod.

Once we get the herd close to the corral, some cow at the last second is usually going to decide to make a break for it, heading back to the fields. We had to stop that breakaway cow or the whole herd quickly follows in a stampeding panic. Doc was convinced that cows were harmless, and that they could be bluffed if he stood his ground. I argued that most could be bluffed, but some could not, just like people. Doc always said I was being a chicken whenever I stepped aside at the last minute and let a cow go through the area I was guarding. "That one would have nailed me," I would say, and he would say, "Nonsense, you just chickened out, you need to hold your ground and call their bluff." So, it was very gratifying during one particular roundup when one of those cows turned toward Doc and not only kept coming, but drove him back ten yards as Doc stayed on his feet, and then slammed him against the side of the barn, trying to crush him with its head. Doc used a pair of pliers that he carried in the outside breast pocket of his blue jean jacket to gouge the cow's eye and back her off. If he hadn't stabbed her eye, he would've have been dead. Even though he had broken ribs, I could not resist saying "Doc, you just need to hold your ground better and call her bluff," which caused him a great deal of pain as he chuckled with broken ribs. The cow lost an eye from the gouging and from then on became known as

“Dead-Eye.” Dead-Eye was one of the cows I knew we had to let through, even before she became Dead-Eye. With only one good eye, she was even more dangerous if she sensed someone was on her blind side. From then on, we tried to leave her out of the roundups. But the lemming factor works both ways, and she usually managed to work her way into the corral.

People are the same way. Stereotypes exist for a reason, but there are always exceptions. I agreed with Doc that 95% of the cows could be bluffed. But if you stood your ground on the 5%, you could be seriously injured. I decided early in life that I could avoid a lot of bad situations if I could spot the 5% outliers along the way. I call it the 5% factor. Same with sharks and grizzlies. I believe that 95% of sharks and grizzlies will leave humans alone. But 5% want to eat me as soon as they see me. So the question becomes, how quickly can I spot the 5%? That is why animal lovers who believe they become friends with wild animals (e.g., the grizzly bear couple) will only live for as long as they don’t encounter the 5% factor. Same for the person who routinely swims with sharks: all fine until Mr. 5% shows up in a gray suit. That is when it is game-over.

Duck Hunting

We had seventy-five head of Black Angus cattle on one hundred acres of beautiful rolling farmland. Ray's Creek, named after the Masters golf course creek, meandered through it, and we had a nice farm pond, perfect size for the property.

The pond froze in the winter, but not safely. In the summer, the cows crowded into the pond to escape the high humidity and cool off. They waded in chest high, and their soaked tails made for effective fly swatters. The pond was loaded with bluegill and bullfrogs. Given that they dug the pond fifty years ago and they never stocked it with fish, how the heck did fish end up in the farm pond? The only thing we could ever think of is that a bird of prey, like a red tailed hawk, lost its grip on a female bluegill with eggs and accidentally dropped it in the pond as it flew over. Later, another bird accidently dropped a male bluegill to fertilize the eggs. Sounds far-fetched, but farm ponds are notorious for never being stocked by the farmer but somehow ending up with fish in them. Either that, or there is a Johnny Appleseed of stocking farm ponds with bluegill, a "Bobby Bluegill," some crazy guy who spends his entire life sneaking into farm ponds across the country at night, dropping in a male and female bluegill that he carries in a bucket as he climbs across barbed wire fences.

We built a rickety plank dock on the pond so we could be above the messy manure-filled mud banks and reach a cane pole line out to the bluegill. How the bluegill survived among all the cow manure, we have no idea. The manure half floated, half sank. Big bullfrogs would jump from floating cowpie to floating cowpie. When a floater was gooey, the frog would disappear into it when it landed on top, go out through the bottom, and then reappear by coming up through another one a few minutes later. Sometimes, the frogs would be stuck in a manure quagmire and struggle for a couple minutes, unsure whether to try to get up on top or go out the bottom. There were big bullfrogs in the pond, and the frog gigging was great. We would attach a barbed trident to a ten-foot bamboo pole, because bamboo was so light-weight it would float if dropped. With an empty potato sack and a flashlight, the idea was to shine the light in the bullfrog's eyes, putting them in a trance. The expression should he "frozen like a bullfrog in a flashlight beam" versus "like a deer in the headlights." Then we would thrust the spear and gig them, aiming just behind the eyes. We would hold the light in one hand and the gig in the other. Or we would tape the flashlight to the bamboo pole; it's a personal gigging preference. It was never easy taking a frog off the gig, as they use their hands and feet like little people and they are rarely killed by being gigged. So we had to grab the frog as he wrapped his hands and feet around our fingers and pushed back with all his might, determined to survive. When we pulled him off the gig with reverse barbs, that bullfrog grimaced like a great actor in a movie having a sword pulled out of his stomach. It is not for the faint of heart or a queasy stomach. They also stay alive in the potato sack, and we have to get them out of the bag at the end of the night to clean them. So we go through the death grip all over again as they push hard on our hands and fingers trying to get away when we pull them out of the potato sack.

We always ate what we killed, except for groundhogs, starlings, crows, sparrows, and snakes. Cleaning bullfrogs is not easy, so giggers have to really like frog legs, which we thankfully did. We used a frog skin peeler to get the frog skin off. Think of the concept of rolling back a tuna can lid with the key. It was pretty amazing to me that someone manufactured a frog skin peeler, and they could be bought at Farm and Fleet, like an Ace Hardware for farmers.

So one day, when I was about ten years old, I'm fishing on the dock at the pond with Grandpa and I'm behind him. We are catching a good amount of bluegill that day. Grandpa reaches back with his cane pole to swing the line out extra far, but when he came through, he hooked me behind my ear. As he gave a lunge to cast the line, he jerked me into the pond from the pull on the back of my ear. Very painful, having a hook in my ear, plus, I landed in the floating cowpies. You never, ever wanted to swim in our pond; it was "cow patty city." By the time I climbed up the muddy manure bank of the pond, I was screaming bloody murder and was covered in cow manure. Not sure which I was crying about more, the hook in my ear or the cowpie swim. We had to walk back to the farmhouse and find a pair of cutting pliers to cut the barb off the hook and then slide the hook from my ear. That was the last time I ever fished with Grandpa. In fact, when I added up haircuts, driving, and now the fishing experience, my new plan was to avoid any private Grandpa interaction at all costs.

The farm pond was also the home of many ducks, and our duck hunting at the pond was very good. When the ducks learned that we were in the trees at one end of the pond, they started coming in on the other side, so we no longer had a shot at them.

This started the game of, "Who is smarter, us or the ducks?" So our next move was to build a "duck blind," to conceal one or more hunters at the other end of the pond, and that assured us another year of good duck hunting. But after one season, the ducks learned what our new blind looked like and they stopped coming in without first checking to see if we were in the blind or the woods. The high, fast fly-overs were able to spot us in the blind or hiding in the trees. They also stopped coming, as if they knew we were hunting them. Doc and I were sitting around in the blind one morning, realizing the ducks had outsmarted us again, when he turned to me and said "What are the ducks not afraid of in the pond?"

"The cows," I answered.

"Right," he said.

We always marveled at the coexistence of the cows and the ducks. The ducks would come dive-bombing into the pond and land very close to the cows, almost landing on top of them. The cows would never so much as flinch, and the ducks never flinched if cows were coming in or out of the water.

"So our blind needs to be a cow," said Doc.

How?" I asked, sensing a big project coming.

"Our duck blind must be a Black Angus cow," Doc repeated. And then I got it. We would build a blind to look like the top half of a Black Angus cow wading in four feet of water. Picture an aerial view of the top half of a cow; it would be the head, neck, back, and tail. The Black Angus cows went in just deep enough to cover their legs and stomach but never the back and tail. They always kept their tail out of the water to swish the flies off their back.

So we built a Black Angus cow out of chicken wire and paper maché, then from that we built a plaster mold and cast it in fiberglass. We stretched a cowhide over the black fiberglass back for authenticity, and we hinged the top so that the top of our cow blind flipped open like the top cover of an old watch and we could come up firing. We cut eyeholes in the head for duck watching, and we were back in action.

We had a great duck season and had clearly outsmarted them. But by the end of that season, somehow they had figured out which Black Angus cow in the pond was not real. How could they be this smart?

We were sitting in the blind one day, getting skunked, and Doc asked, "What is our fake cow not doing that all the other live cows in the pond are doing?"

"Our cow is not swishing its tail at flies, it's not taking a dump, and it's not twitching its ears," I answered.

"Exactly," Doc said.

So then we made a 5-foot tail from a large black garden hose, put chicken wire in it to reinforce it, with an authentic bushy tail on the very end (from the cow graveyard). We bought a dozen small brown footballs and a dozen small brown Frisbees. We filled the small footballs half full of water so they would bob and semi-float like a real cow patty. Then we cut a hole just below the tail for the cow patty release. We put my little sister in the back of the cow, and we dubbed her the Tail Swisher and Cowpie Queen. She would alternate between chucking out a small brown football or a small brown Frisbee, simulating the two common shapes of cow dumps. Then she would swish the tail. For twitching ears, we used drumsticks and glued cow ears (also from the cow graveyard) on the ends of each drumstick. Next, we cut ear holes, and then had my other little sister positioned in the head of our cow. We nicknamed her the "Air Traffic Controller," since she would make similar hand motions with the drumsticks to make the ears twitch. As ducks approached, one sister would be sitting in the head of the cow and twitch the ear drumsticks back and forth, while the other would work the back end. With both sisters working the front and back, we were back in business, fooling the ducks again, and we had another record season.

Duck Plucker

After a duck hunt, we must clean the ducks before we freeze them. But ducks are tough to clean, and those feathers that protect them from the frigid winter waters are extremely hard to remove. It takes a long time to pluck a duck by hand, and thus, from the beginning of time, duck hunters have sought to come up with a better way to "pluck the duck."

Doc and I decided to build a duck plucker. We had seen several over the years, and we borrowed design elements from the best of what was out there. We used an old Jeep motor and horizontally mounted a steel drum barrel. We put one hundred holes in the barrel, just big enough to fit a piece of garden hose snugly. We took 4-inch pieces of the hose, with a diagonal cut at the end of each piece, and jammed the pieces into the holes. We adjusted the hose pieces so all the slanted ends were facing the same direction. We mounted the barrel sideways on this old Jeep chassis, so when we hit the gas pedal, the barrel spun. We could control the speed of the barrel spin by the gas pedal.

Then, we held the duck with two hands and pushed the duck against the spinning barrel. The slanted garden hose pieces knocked the feathers off the duck. Once we were finished with one side, we flipped the duck over and did the other side.

A duck breast is tough enough to withstand the pressure, unless the duck is hit at close range. The person operating the duck plucker must be able to tell how badly the duck was hit in the chest, and apply the right amount of pressure accordingly. Beginners working the machine would push too hard and send the whole duck flying off the machine. Push down too lightly, and the feathers won't come off. Push too hard on a duck that had been shot at close range, and you blow the duck breast meat into pieces and have nothing left to eat.

We put an old outhouse hut over the duck plucker machine, with a small window to let in some light. We decided that Granny would be an excellent duck plucker. She lived with us, and Doc was always looking for ways to put her to work. This seemed like the perfect role for her, and she became "Madame Duck Plucker."

In her early attempts, Granny pushed too hard on ducks and sent them flying right through the small window. We boarded up the window and ran electricity out to the hut so we could hang a light bulb in the rafters over the duck plucker. That made it warmer in the winter, and provided the necessary light. It was still pretty dim in there, and hard to see. Stray barn cats quickly learned to come into the duck plucker with Granny when it was plucking time, since they could sit up in the rafters of the hut and wait for a duck that had been shot at close range to be pushed too hard against the plucker. The breast meat would blow apart and the barrel would spin duck guts up onto the ceiling, and the rafters were close enough to the ceiling to allow the stray cats to reach up for a special treat and stay warm near the ceiling because of the light bulb. Granny liked the cats and always let them into the hut to pluck ducks with her.

We outfitted Granny with a chef's apron, rubber gloves to protect her fingers, and shop goggles. While tentative at first, she became extremely proficient and impressed us all with her speed. She quickly developed a sense of pride in her duck-plucking operation. Even though she could not see very well, she could clean six ducks in five minutes and she was getting faster every day.

One day after we had knocked down a dozen ducks, we told Granny we needed her to clean them. She looked at her watch and told us she had promised my mom to go into town with her in five minutes. She quickly donned her chef apron, goggles, and gloves, then headed out to the plucker shed. Two barn cats followed her in as she shut the door behind her, and the cats quickly climbed up to their perch just above her shoulder. The ceiling was probably six feet tall, and Granny was around five-feet-five inches, so the cats were very close. Granny was cranking through those ducks when we heard a horrific wail come from the Duck Plucker shed, like a child with her fingers caught in a car door. In Granny's haste to clean those ducks quickly, she had accidentally overreached the duck pile and had grabbed a barn cat by mistake. With all the feathers flying and the dim light, it was easy to envision how she could overreach the duck pile. It all happened so fast. She had laid the cat down against the duck plucker on its back and burned the hair off the back of the cat. That was when the cat let out a mighty scream.

The rubber gloves were protecting Granny from the sharp claws that the cat used to try to get free from Granny's grasp. She then flipped the cat over and nailed its stomach to the duck plucker, causing another scream to come from the hut. Then she tossed the "duck" into her "clean" pile on the other side, oblivious to the fact that she had just burned the hair off both sides of a cat. We came running when we heard the screams.

We opened the door and the stunned cat staggered out, wobbling from pain and weakness. We took the female cat to the barn and put white cow salve on the burned skin. Because it was an all-black female cat, the white salve made the cat look like a skunk.

"The cat will live," said a relieved Doc. We named her Skunky, and nine months later we discovered the first known litter of "skunk cats" on our farm. They were more nimble and faster than a skunk, able to climb trees like a cat, but with the ability to spray if cornered. We could only imagine the courtship that Mr. Pepé Le Pew, a big male skunk, must have put on that cat. The skunk-cats ("skats" we called them, since "cunks" was a bit risky to say) all eventually disappeared from the farm.

Granny's Retail Duck Business

Before retiring to Martin Meadows, Granny was head of the food service program at Ohio State University. Her favorite part of the job was the athletic training table. Basketball was her favorite sport to watch, so she took particular interest in the basketball team. Her favorite team was the 1962 National Champs, with Jerry Lucas, John Havlicek, and Bobby Knight. She received Christmas cards for years from these three, and she loved those guys. We had a ninetieth birthday party at the farm for her, and Jerry Lucas, who was from Middletown, was kind enough to come back for the celebration. At this stage, he had achieved riches and fame from his memory book and memory system after a highly successful NBA career. When I was a senior in high school, he came back to Middletown High School to describe the new memory system to a packed auditorium. After a fascinating presentation on his memory system to the entire high school, he asked the audience if there were any questions. I cracked up the auditorium by raising my hand and asking, "Yeah, uh, what was your name again?"

Since we had lots of ducks, Granny opened a retail duck store out on the highway to sell the extra ducks from our duck hunting. Doc told Granny that she could keep any profit that she made from selling ducks. She would sell live winged ducks that could be used to start a duck breeding operation, and she sold dead ducks that were already plucked, frozen, and ready for the dinner table.

She started her own duck breeding operation in an abandoned corn silo. The corn silo had a concrete floor with a wrap-around wire cylinder that went up twenty-five feet. If the wounded ones recovered and were able to take flight, they could fly in circles up to the top and strengthen their wings. This lead to a third market, selling fully recovered ducks to hunting clubs. The irony was that we would shoot a duck, accidentally wing it, and let it heal just so that hunters at a hunting club could shoot at it again. We set up a duck trap to catch live ducks on the pond, but ducks are smarter than lobsters. Lobsters cannot find their way back to the hole in the lobster trap because they can't look up, and the hole is above them. Ducks can look up, so if they get in, they can get out. The corn silo's poured concrete floor prevented weasels, skunks, foxes, raccoons, badgers, and possums from entering and killing the ducks at night. Most people don't realize that raccoons, skunks, and possums are carnivorous when given the chance. Black snakes would crawl in and grab the eggs, but the ducks all learned to attack a snake together and drive it out. The corn silo was more secure than the chicken coop because of the concrete floor.

Granny painted a big sign that read, "Ducks for Sale" and put it out on the highway. Most people who stopped were simply curious to see if we really were selling ducks. Demand was high around Easter for baby ducks. Like most pets, other than cats and dogs, ducks are cute for about one week, and after that they are very loud, and a smelly mess. They crap all over the place, just like chickens, and they are never quiet. We used a room in the farmhouse for the baby ducks and baby chickens, to keep them warm and alive until they were old enough to be moved to the duck silo or the chicken coop. This room was called the "Chicken Room." It smelled foul, as chicken and duck poop is very high in nitrate, with a strong ammonia smell.

The duck-plucking and duck-breeding operation meant a lot to Granny's psyche to feel useful, valued, and running a business again. So one day, this guy drives up and looks at the ducks in the silo. I'm there helping Granny as her duck retriever. As soon as someone requests a live duck, I take a net and go into the duck silo to catch a duck and bring it out.

This guy says to Granny, "I would like to buy a Pennsylvania duck."

Granny gives me a wink and sends me into the silo to catch a "Pennsylvania" duck. I catch the first one I can, and bring it out, smiling, as I say, "This one is from Pennsylvania."

Granny puts it on the counter and says "That will be five dollars please."

"Not so fast," says the odd fellow. He asks my Granny to turn the duck around so the tail is facing him on the counter. He then says, "Please hold the duck tightly," and he proceeds to wiggle his fingers up the back end of that duck.

The duck lets out a mighty squawk! The odd fellow then removes his fingers, much to the happiness of the duck, and he shakes his head and says, "No, ma'am, that duck is not from Pennsylvania."

"Okay," says Granny, as she hands the duck back to me and says, "You got the wrong one. Get the one from Pennsylvania," with a wink.

So we repeat the process, and again he inserts his fingers up the back of the duck. "Not from Pennsylvania," he asserts.

"We will try once more to get the right duck" Granny says to me, now running out of patience with this "quack."

I retrieve another duck, and this time he smiles as the duck squawks for dear life and his fingers retract from the duck. He says, "Now that is a Pennsylvania duck!"

"Yes, sir!" exclaims my Granny, "That'll be nine dollars for that duck."

"I thought you said five dollars for a duck," said the stranger.

"Pennsylvania ducks cost four dollars more," said Granny. As he was paying, he said, "It sure is nice to finally have a bona fide duck seller in these parts; where exactly are you from?"

And with that question, Granny spins around and turns her back to the man, bends over forward at the waist and throws her skirt up over her back and says, "Go ahead, you tell me!"

Once folks realized we sold ducks, they started asking us if we sold other animals. We would sell a Black Angus and the occasional mean pony, and every once in a while a hunting dog that refused to hunt.

But one day, this guy drives up and asks if we sell black

snakes. Seizing on a business opportunity, Granny says, "Sure we do, but we don't keep them in stock, we catch them once we have an order. And they are five dollars per snake."

The guy explains that he has multiple gardens, but the mice are wreaking havoc in the gardens. Because it is a new development with no woods around, there are no black snakes in his gardens to control the field mice. We tell him to come back in three days, and we will have four black snakes for him. Then I go ask Doc how I'm going to catch four black snakes, given that they hide pretty darn well.

"Easy," he says, "with mice. First we need to catch live field mice. That means we build a live mousetrap. Then we catch the snakes with the live mice."

So first he builds a better mousetrap. He lays an old tin coffee can on its side, with the lid removed. He secures a mousetrap to the front of the coffee can, like a platform sticking out of the front on the bottom of the can. He affixes a piece of screen mesh on top of the mousetrap lever arm, so that when the mouse eats the cheese, he is sitting on a four inch by four inch piece of wire mesh. When the mouse eats the cheese and triggers the trap, the mousetrap spring throws the mouse from the screen platform into the horizontal coffee can and seals the can shut with the rectangular piece of screen.

We built four of them and placed them out in the garden that night. The next morning, we have four live field mice, each trapped in a separate coffee can. Now we take the thinnest wire one can buy, and while holding the mouse with gloves, we tie the wire to his back foot. We place each mouse in the garden that night with a three-foot length of thin wire tied to a stake. When the black snake swallows the mouse, the snake can't get away since he can't bite through the wire or regurgitate the mouse until it is digested. The next morning, we have four black snakes on four wires.

A day later, we pull the half-digested mouse out of the snakes and we drop the four snakes into a potato sack for the customer. And thus we launch our retail black snake operation.

Granny goes out and changes the sign so it reads, "Ducks and Snakes For Sale." But then we decide to make a new sign to include everything; that way, we can get rid of all wounded, crippled, sick, or ineffective animals. So the new sign now reads, "Ducks, Chickens, Sheep, Pigs, Cows, Snakes, Ponies, and Hunting Dogs for Sale," but it's too crammed onto the sign, so we flip the sign over and write, "Animals and Reptiles for Sale." It was amazing how many people now stopped. We started selling box turtles as pets, since one of our dogs, a Springer Spaniel, was amazing at finding them and bringing them up to the farm house. We carved the date into the bottom of the turtle and released it to see if we caught the same turtle again. When we realized people wanted to buy them as pets, we stopped carving dates into their belly shell. The problem is that we could never get the box turtles to eat in captivity. The rumor was that they would eat raw hamburger, but that made no sense to us, since they didn't eat that in the wild, and they were not carnivores. If we caught live flies, they never touched them. What the heck did these turtles eat? We never had one die, but we never saw one eat. Luckily, they are hardy survivors.

My son wanted a box turtle, so my wife bought him one at the pet shop, since we live in Chicago and not close to woods. The pet shop told us to feed it meat pellets. Why meat pellets, if they cannot eat meat in the wild? That still made no sense to me.

This poor turtle doesn't eat for a year, but doesn't die. We finally take it back to the pet shop, and the new pet storeowner explains that it is an Asian Box Turtle, which should spend three-quarters of its life in water and eat fruits and vegetables. Two years of meat pellets, and no water to swim in; how's that for accidentally torturing an animal? It looked the same after it swam and ate strawberries for a year. We once lost two pet snakes in our house and we found one alive a year later, with no food for a year. Reptiles clearly have unbelievable survival abilities without food or water.

Meanwhile, back at the farm, we had some very strange people come by requesting some very strange animals as a result of our sign out by the highway.

A guy comes by one day and asks if he can buy some moles.

"Why would you want to buy moles?" we ask.

He says he wants to use them to loosen up an old piece of ground that he wants to convert to a garden.

So what the heck, we decide to breed some moles. We tell him to come back in four days and we will sell him four live moles. First, we need to build a better mole trap to catch live moles. So we start with a traditional mole death trap and convert it to a live mole trap. We follow the mousetrap conversion technique. Doc specializes in creating live animal traps, and he always starts with the existing death product. The existing mole product is a guillotine-type box contraption with spikes that are spring-loaded. The spikes drive down through the mole when the mole steps on the platform underground. The trap looks like a five-inch square mini-elevator with two open walls and two lateral closed walls, a floor, and a ceiling. In the ceiling are several five-inch long spikes ready to plunge down through the open space as soon as a mole steps on the platform and triggers the spikes. It was a contraption right out of an Indiana Jones movie. The traps are buried along one of the mole's tunnel routes, with the open sides aligned with the tunnel so the mole can step into his death chamber. So, Doc simply saws off and removes the spikes, adds two new sides that drop down when the mole steps onto the platform, and voilà, a live mole trap. So we start catching and selling live moles, plus we started breeding them for bigger and better moles.

Granny had already won ribbons at the Ohio State Fair for largest zucchini and pumpkin, so why couldn't she breed the largest mole? Sister Molly had a steer win at The Ohio State Fair so we got her involved as well. After several years of breeding,

Granny ends up with a very large stud male mole that she names Black Magic, and he was the size of a Cocker Spaniel. She put it next to the stall where we kept our prized sow pig, Big Betty. The pig was kept in the stall so she did not get pregnant from our boar. We want to show the pig at the Ohio State Fair, but we don't want Big Betty to get pregnant and miss the fair. If the big queen sow is delivering babies, she will not be able to make the trip to Columbus. Granny believes the pig, Betty, can win "Biggest in State." So this female pig, Betty, is in heat right next to the stall where we put Black Magic. The problem is that we underestimated Black Magic. Black Magic spends the night burrowing under the stall separating him from Big Betty. The next morning, Doc finds him in the stall with the female sow, and both are exhausted. Nine months later, the sow gives birth to these pig-like furry creatures who can see equally well above or below the ground, during day or night, can dig tunnels like crazy, and are half the size of pigs. We called them "Ground Hogs," and now they are all over the Midwest. We kept the first offspring as a pet and named her Black Betty, as tribute to her parents Black Magic and Big Betty.

A local rock band was so impressed with the story that they wrote a song about that first groundhog named Black Betty. Later, a more famous rocker, Huddie Ledbetter, stole the song and made it big, with the chorus line of "Whoa-oh Black Betty, Bam-a-Lam."

Old Folks Home

Just down the road from the Martin Meadows on Route 4 was a retirement home called Garden Manor. Occasionally we would catch an old guy wandering onto our farm, and he was always an escapee from the old folks home. Doc buried a can of peas on the back forty, claiming that if we ever put him in the home, he would escape and live off the can of peas that he would dig up. One day, Doc is scoping the farm for groundhogs to shoot when he sees an old guy stuck on one of our fences back in the far corner of our property. We get into the pickup truck and ride out to get him. His legs are locked up, so he is stuck straddling the fence. Doc lifts him while I pry his cramped legs off the fence. We put him in the pickup and start a conversation, asking him where he is headed.

"Chicago," he replies.

"Aren't you from Garden Manor?" Doc asks.

"What's that?" he replies.

Doc and I look at each other; we still assume he is from the retirement home.

As we drive up the driveway to Garden Manor, he says "Nice place you have here," so we are now starting to actually worry he may not be from the retirement home.

There is a pond in the front of the building, and as we get out of the truck, he points to the ducks on the pond and says, "Where'd you get the ducks?"

Now Doc and I are really unsure where he came from. We go up and ring the doorbell to the home anyway, and a nurse steps out. She immediately recognizes our guy, rushing toward him.

"Mr. Johnson, you had us all scared to death with your escape!"

"I almost had these guys fooled," he said with a smile, as the nurse leads him back into the home.

Granny's White Glove Train Ride

Granny used to take the train from Columbus to Middletown to visit us before she moved to Martin Meadows. She always dressed up for the train ride and wore white gloves. She was on the train one day, seated next to the window, with a businessman in a white shirt and suit seated next to her in the aisle seat. She excused herself to visit the washroom, and the man had to get up so she could go to the woman's room on the train. When she came back, he was asleep in the aisle seat. She thought she could squeeze by his knees to her seat without waking him. She was holding her white gloves in her hand along with her purse as she started sliding past his knees. The train suddenly lurched and she reached for the rail on top of the seat to regain her balance. In the process she dropped one of her white gloves on the man's crotch. She squeezed by him and sat back in her seat, and thought about how she might retrieve the glove, when the train rocked a bit more. The man half-opened his eyes and saw what he thought was his white shirttail protruding from his pants zipper. In a dazed-sleep state, he reached down, undid his pants zipper, and stuffed her white glove into his pants. Then he zipped his pants up and went back to sleep.

Mortified, Granny never had the courage to tell him what he did, but always wondered what he (or his wife) must have thought as he took his suit pants off later that night.

Visa Card

Later in life, Granny started running up a big Visa card bill by ordering the stuff she saw marketed on television. We had no idea she was buying everything she saw. Doc finally saw one of her Visa bills and the interest charges and called up Visa. He explained that she was old, she was not aware of what she was doing, and the interest charges were obscene. Doc explained that he would pay for all the actual purchases if Visa would reverse out all the interest charges.

When the customer service rep said they would not be willing to do that, Doc said, "Well, now I'm going to use her as collateral for the bill. Here is the address, Visa can come get her!" and he hung up the phone. The next Visa bill that came in the mail had dropped all the interest charges and Doc paid the bill.

As Granny started to pass gas at the dinner table on a regular basis, he would say, "The dog must have just run through the room." If she let out a loud blast at the dinner table, he would grab his napkin and cover his face like he was trying to survive tear gas, and dive under the dinner table exclaiming, "Tell me when it's safe!" and we kids would have to bite our lip, trying to contain ourselves but unable to maintain composure. Granny wasn't amused.

Field Trial

We always trained hunting dogs, and Doc wanted to see how good some of his dogs really were. The only way to test them was in competition against other hunting dogs, known as Field Trial Competition (FTC). Some of our best hunting dogs were not trainable for Field Trial since they had been hunting with us for too long, but he took a young English Setter, named Blue, and decided to focus on Field Trial with him. This meant whistle commands, hand signals, and the need for us to be on horseback to keep up with the dog during the competition.

I was fourteen when we entered Blue in his first FTC. Since we worried about controlling our own horses because they were too wild, we had the option of renting horses from the FTC that were supplied by local horse owners. The other reason we wanted to rent their horses was that we had multiple bad experiences with trailering our horses and cows. We didn't want to trailer our own horses. We got there, and I ended up with a monster of a horse that proved to be far too much for me to handle right off the bat.

The idea is that all the judges, plus the dog owners, follow the dog on horseback. The owner provides the whistle commands to guide the dog around the course, where quail and pheasant have been hidden. The dogs score points every time they successfully point, hold, and then flush the bird on command. When the dog stops and points, the owner then dismounts and shoots the bird after commanding his dog to flush it. Then the dog retrieves the shot bird, bringing it back to the owner, scoring more points. Of course, the horse needs to be trained to stay calm around a shotgun blast, another big problem if we used our own horses.

We tried it with our horses on our own farm, but ended up on the ground with the horses in the next county. The first time we both fired shotguns from horseback, we were thrown "Hi-ho, Silver!" style. We gave up trying to shoot from the horse, and next tried to teach the horses to stay calm if we shot near them (that didn't work either).

Back to FTC, the dog with the most points after going once around the course wins. There are multiple dog-and-owner teams on the course at one time. The course is spread across several hundred acres of land to allow the competition to happen all in one day. The course must be completed within a specific time allotment as well.

We get ready, and the judge starts the stopwatch and says, "Begin!"

Blue takes off down a mowed strip in the middle of a field, and this strip acts as a natural "road" for the dog and riders to follow. Fifty yards down the strip, Blue takes an unexpected hard left into the brush. We dog owners all know roughly where the birds are positioned, and this is way too close to the start for there to be a bird station. Doc and I go charging after him on our horses, with Doc blowing his whistle hard and yelling for Blue to stop. We are halfway toward another group of competitors when Blue stops and turns around and starts coming back toward us. The problem is that I cannot stop my horse. My horse has moved into a gallop, and while I have pulled his head back, we are heading quickly toward the group of competitors as Blue goes whizzing by me in the opposite direction. I pull on the reins with all my might; he gives a buck and knocks me up onto his neck, up and out of the saddle. Now I'm holding on for dear life to his neck, and we go charging right through a competitor's bird position, and the quail go flying everywhere. The horse runs me wild through two more bird positions before a judge is able to ride up alongside and stop my horse with me clinging to its neck. My horse and I have single-handedly destroyed half the entire competition for the afternoon. The judge guides my horse back to the start, and informs us that we are not only disqualified, we are banned from any future Field Trial Competition in the area for a full year.

That was the first and last field trial experience for me. To add insult to injury, Doc put his hat down (he always wore a Stetson) to pack up our gear, and Blue was within reach on a chain. Blue trotted over and promptly peed on his hat, causing him to bellow at Blue and smack the dog with his pee-covered hat. I laughed hard inside, but my uncontrolled horse had caused too much damage for me to laugh out loud.

Blue ended up being a worthless hunting dog, as worthless as he was at field trial, so we decided to sell him. He never followed our commands, so I was curious as to how we could impress a potential buyer. The first potential buyer showed up at Martin Meadows and asked for a demonstration of his capabilities. Doc sent Blue out into the field and when he was forty yards out, Doc blew his whistle for Blue to head to the left, and *damn* if Blue didn't head left! Then Doc blew his whistle for Blue to come back toward us, and Blue headed back toward us. Blue followed each command perfectly. Doc and I stared at each other in complete disbelief, as Blue had never done this before. Doc immediately doubled the price of the dog to $200, but the buyer reminded us of the price in the paper at $100. Doc got an extra $50 and that was the last we ever heard of Blue, but we are convinced he is still out there busting up field trials somewhere.

Mom's Horse

My mom had a favorite horse named Brandy, a dark brown chestnut mare bigger than Secretariat, the famous Kentucky Derby Champion. We never officially measured the horse; we just told everyone that Brandy was bigger than Secretariat. My wife's brother Dave was a crazy Marine who visited Martin Meadows for a fall weekend. He had watched one too many Western movies, and he climbed a tree and sat out on a limb, waiting for one of our horses to walk underneath the limb. There was a well-worn path under the limb, since a butt-bag holding white fly repellant also hung from the limb for the horses and cows. Brandy wandered under the limb, and David dropped out of the tree onto her back. She panicked and took off straight for a hill, wet from a recent rain. She lost her footing down the hill on a dead run and fell with two-hundred-twenty-pound David whooping and hollerin' on her back. She broke her hip in a tumbling fall, and David was lucky the horse didn't kill him. David walked back to the farmhouse and told us what happened, and explained that the horse is back up on its feet but can't walk.

Doc goes out to check the horse and can immediately tell that Brandy must be put down. He goes in and gets his pistol, loading his old .45 from the Korean War. He puts the pistol behind his back and walks out to the horse. When he gets within twelve feet, he is about to take the pistol from behind his back and shoot her in the head when she smells the gun. How the horse knew she was going to be shot, we will never know. But she took off with the broken hip, careening across the field. She somehow half-jumped and half-fell over a fence with a broken hip onto the neighbor's property.

So Doc backed off and went to the farmhouse for his deer rifle. Brandy made it on three legs into the neighboring farmer's vegetable garden, breathing hard. Doc shot her from two-hundred-fifty yards away, standing on our property. The horse staggered and keeled over dead in the middle of their vegetable garden. Doc walked back home and blankly stated, "Not good."

The neighboring farmer, Mr. Morgan, called an hour later and said, "There is a dead horse in my vegetable garden," and Doc said, with an air of disbelief, "Why would you let a horse into your vegetable garden?"

Morgan yelled, "I know it's gotta be yours, since your cows are constantly breaking into my corn fields, so why wouldn't your dead horse be in my vegetable garden?!!"

Doc said, "What color is the horse?"

Morgan yelled into the phone, "You know damn well what color the horse is!!"

Doc said, "I'm looking out at my horses and the only one I don't see is a black one (the dead horse is brown)."

The farmer screamed into the phone "Get this f***ing dead horse off my property!"

"I would if it was mine, but it must be yours. Sorry for your loss," and hung up.

To this day, that neighbor works himself into a state of rage whenever anyone mentions Doc's name.

Dove Hunting

Right next door to our farm is the Morgan Farm. One of our fields borders the Morgans' stand of pine trees. We assumed the Morgans never cared if we hunted there, or at least, they never came out when they heard us blasting away.

The doves would eat in our cornfields all day, swing by the farm pond at dusk for water, and then come swooping into the pines like Japanese dive-bombers to roost for the night. It was great fun and a real challenge to shoot them before they reached the pines, and we loved to eat doves. The State of Ohio later eliminated the dove season, but we decided to not officially recognize the moratorium and we continued to hunt them.

One day, we had Bill Verity, Chairman of Armco Steel Corporation, which was headquartered in our town, and his son, Will, out for a hunt. It was a great afternoon of hunting and the doves were flying in hot and heavy.

At one point Bill yells to my dad, "Hey Doc, I have fifteen doves so far, what's the limit?" and my dad yells back, "No limit!" and we all keep shooting.

As the sun goes down, we stop shooting when we can't see them coming in anymore and head back to the farmhouse to clean them. It's a very successful hunt. We are cleaning lots of doves, drinking beer, very happy about a great hunt, and Bill says, "This is the greatest fun, and I can't believe there's no limit."

Doc, without even looking up from his dove cleaning, says, "No season either."

Bill's jaw drops to the floor, and then he laughs hard and asks if he and Will can come back and hunt the next weekend. Doc explains that we won't be there, but they are welcome to come back anytime.

We have a farmhand, Pat, who stays in the tenant house, and we forget to tell Pat that Bill and his son might be coming out to shoot doves the next weekend.

So Bill and Will come out the next Saturday afternoon and start blasting away back in the Morgan pine trees. Our farmhand Pat hears them and calls the sheriff. The sheriff shows up and walks out to the pines where they are just slaying the doves.

"What do you think you are doing?" asks the sheriff.

"We have permission from the owner, Dr. Ted Martin, to hunt here," says Bill.

"Well, you two are in serious trouble," responds the officer.

"One, you're hunting on Morgan's land, not Martin's land, and Mr. Morgan has been calling us for years complaining about the Martins hunting in his pine trees."

We have failed to mention to the Veritys that the pines are not actually on our property.

"Second, if there was a dove season, you would be hunting out of season. But there is no dove season. Therefore, you don't have a hunting license, either."

Bill is getting really nervous and says, "I'm Bill Verity,

chairman of Armco Steel; let's work this out together."

The sheriff scoffs, "Yeah, and I'm Richard Nixon, the President of the United States, now let's go take a walk to the squad car."

When they get back to the cars, Bill pulls out his driver's license and hands it to the sheriff. The sheriff looks at the license with a look of shock and says, "Mr. Verity, thank you for hiring me. I work part time at night at your steel mill. Here is your license back, have a nice day," and drives off.

There are some benefits to small town living.

Once, we were cleaning a pile of quail, and we were marveling at how full the crop (the see-through area above the stomach) was in each bird, full of whole kernels of yellow field corn. We would poke the crop with a knife and send the corn scattering around the newspapers.

My younger sister, Mol, a five-year-old, liked to watch us clean the birds. Suddenly, we hear her, "Ptttt, Pshttt," as she spits out several kernels of corn. She was picking them up from the newspaper and eating them, but since they were field corn, the kernels were way too hard for her to chew.

Mol would also feed her ponytail to one of our goats. She had a long ponytail that she would braid, and one day she was leaning over the fence and the goat started swallowing her ponytail. She figured out she could feed the entire two foot long ponytail to the goat and then pull it out of the goat's stomach. Doc saw this and it gave him the inspiration for catching snakes.

Practical Jokes

We liked to have families out to the farm as guests, but we also liked to play practical jokes on them while they were visiting. Many never came back as a result.

One of our favorites was the "Hog Waller." The hogs like to congregate at the lowest point of the farm, where a mix of mud, hog manure, and hog slop would form a bog where somebody could sink in up to his waist. It was surrounded by normal pasture. The surface was slightly lower than the surrounding ground, but it was like quicksand if anyone fell into it. As guests arrived, we would start talking about the great tradition of an old-fashioned footrace. We had a running course all marked out, a quarter-mile loop around the nearest field, so everyone who was not participating could watch the footrace. If guests were coming out on Saturday afternoon, we would spend the morning covering the Hog Waller with grass, straw and chaff. Then we would mark the footrace course so it went right across the covered Hog Waller. We had it perfectly camouflaged, so it blended in with the surrounding field. We waited for all the guests to arrive and then we would start "selling" the footrace. Everyone was in. We went to the starting line, and then had someone say "Go," and we would let our guests move nicely out in front. Halfway around the course, the first guest would hit the covered Hog Waller, and end up launching into a Superman dive with a full face plant into the bog, almost disappearing from sight before standing up covered head to foot in hog manure. They were always in disbelief at what had just happened. Sometimes, two or three would go in if it was a close race and they were tightly bunched at the front of the pack. Everyone else would laugh so hard that they had tears coming down their cheeks. Many never came back once they figured out it was a camouflaged set-up and had been planned out in advance.

Another practical joke was to tell one of my friends that he needed to go into the stall and pin the small steer down on the ground so we could ear-tag it. The steer never was a big one, maybe it came up to our waist, but three hundred pounds, all muscle, was impossible to pin. So we would tell a football player to casually hop in there and pin down that steer for us. One, he would have trouble catching the steer, and two, when he cornered it, the steer would blow right through him. Meanwhile, he would get battered, bruised, and humiliated until we burst out laughing and Doc told him, "No one can flip that steer over without tying up the feet rodeo-style."

The practical jokes also occurred inside Doc's own family when he was growing up. His sister Marty went away to summer Girl Scout camp for two weeks. She loved her brown and white horse at the farm, an Appaloosa named Spark. So Doc decides to paint the horse solid black the day before she got back from summer camp. When she arrived home and looked for her horse, she saw several horses, but not hers. She ran crying to her parents that her horse was gone. People said a horse could die if it was painted, but her horse was fine. It did take a year for the paint to grow out, so for a long time the horse was black, brown, and white. His sister was not amused.

Growing up on the farm, horseback riding was like getting on a live roller coaster, one that was all uphill the first half and all downhill the second half. We did not ride the horses enough for them to be well trained, so they were wild. We purposely misnamed the horses. We named the two wildest ones "Cupcake" and "Bread Dough," and we named the calmer ones "Dynamite" and "Firecracker." This was Doc's sense of humor at it again. He would ask a guest which horse they would like to ride by name, and they always picked Cupcake or Bread Dough. Once anyone put on the saddle, the horse would swell up like a pufferfish. The horse knew how to bloat, and had to be caught off guard with a knee to the belly to get them to exhale so the cinch belt could be tightened sufficiently. Otherwise, the saddle seemed on tight, but the horse knew the rider would be slipping sideways as soon as it relaxed its bloated stomach in mid-run. This happened to more than one guest. Guest "Bobba Louie" actually held on after his saddle slipped, clinging like a spider monkey as he rode back to the barn underneath his horse.

We always had to watch out for the "butt bags" when riding. Butt bags are bags of white fly repellant hanging from tree limbs, so the cows could butt the bags with their heads, dispensing sticky white flour-like powder on their head to repel black flies.

We would get on the horses at the barn, and then fight to make them go into the far back corner of the farm. Once we reached the back corner, they would be ready to turn like a quarter horse turning around a barrel, heading back to the barn. Then it was time to hold on for dear life, no steering required. It was an adrenaline rush and a fifty-fifty chance of making it back without getting tossed. And talk about "coming in hot" back at the barn! More than once, the horse couldn't stop soon enough and slid through the barn and out the other side, assuming both doors were open. One day, the far-side sliding aluminum barn door was closed and my horse slammed into the door with a big chest thump, bending the tracks at the top of the sliding frame door so it would never open again.

"What the Sam Hell are you doing?" Doc yelled.

"Ask the horse, not me," I replied.

Our original barn was a classic old structure with multiple levels, built by family in the eighteen-hundreds. It burned down in 1968 in a terrible fire. We got all the animals out, but there was no way to stop the inferno. We don't know if some kids might have been smoking in the barn, or whether a mouse chewed through an old wire. Doc rebuilt an aluminum barn, and put an Armco steel sticker on the barn, implying it was made of steel. That was his sense of humor, tweaking the Armco guys that their steel was like aluminum.

We would instruct the guests on horseback to make sure

they knew not to let their horse turn its head until we said it was time to turn them. When we were two hundred yards from the back corner of the farm, Doc would say, "Now get ready to hang on for dear life, 'cause there is no stopping the race that is about to begin. When your horse veers toward the butt bags, stretch your head down low and forward on the horse's neck so the butt bag glances off your back."

Then I would say, "Or else shift out of the saddle "Indian style" until you are hanging on the side of the horse, and then swing yourself back up into the saddle after your horse goes under the bag."

Doc failed to tell them that this was going to happen while the horse was on a dead run.

At this point the guests are scared and they are almost to the back corner. I add to the fear by telling tell them that I suggest they forget about the reins, double-hold the saddle horn, and swing their stirrups forward *if* they make it to the barn so they don't get thrown over the front of the horse when the horse puts on the brakes in the barn.

The guests are now terrified. We reach the back corner and all four horses wheel as if they have been stung by hornets and break into a dead run back for the barn.

Most guests did not survive the crossing of Ray's Creek, or the sharp turn after the creek, and those that did usually came out white as ghosts from the butt bag powder right after the creek crossing. At Ray's Creek, the horse would take a leap at the creek, which pitched the rider backward. Then the horse landed and the rider got slammed forward onto the neck of the horse. Before the rider could regain his balance, the horse made a sharp left up the hill and the rider was now thrown off to the right. If the rider was off balance, but still on from the sharp left, the butt bag knocked him off. Cupcake and Bread Dough would run at full speed right at the butt bag and duck under at the last second. The rider would take a full hit and come out covered like a snowball. Very few ever made it all the way back to the barn. The amazing observation in hindsight is that we never had a serious injury in over a dozen "tosses" (although our friend Dougie's daughter broke her arm).

Travelall

Doc had a 1972 Travelall, the first and only consumer SUV that International Harvester ever made. It looked like a cross between a H3 Hummer and a Suburban, and it was solid steel. The doors weighed two times what doors weigh today. We put up a Barrie-Aire Pet Barrier, a dog cage fence to keep the dogs in the way back and keep them from hopping over the back seat. We would travel a very hilly road to Uncle Fred's farm outside of Trenton for dove hunting. Doc would be driving, and as we approached the roller coaster of upcoming hills, he would get a glimmer in his eye. If we had a new dove hunter (like Kip) in the back seat, Doc and I would quietly attach our waist seatbelts. The guest would never have a seatbelt on in the back seat, no one ever did. There were no shoulder belts back then, either. Doc would hit the first hill and the guest would get launched to the ceiling of the Travelall, head smacking against the roof, and come slamming back down. This process would repeat over every hill and we would have tears rolling down our cheeks at the expression on the guests' faces. We stapled a sheet of Styrofoam to the inside roof of the Travelall above the dogs so the dogs wouldn't hurt themselves when they were launched upward. No one ever got hurt and the hills happened so quickly in succession that they never had a chance of finding the seatbelts after the first hill.

Pigup

As a teenager, my friend Rick and I would try to "borrow" the biggest pig in the area, if we had nothing else to do on a Saturday night. If we got one, we would then deliver that pig to someone's back yard in the middle of the night. It was an innocent prank in theory, since the farmer called the sheriff the next day. We always left a note at the farm missing the pig that said, "Call the sheriff to find your pig," and we always wrote a note on the pig with a magic marker that said, "Call the sheriff to have me picked up."

And thus, it was easy for the sheriff to put two pieces of the puzzle together and inform the owner where to retrieve his pig. To hijack a pig, we cut a large piece of plywood that would fit into the back bed of the pickup truck. We doubled it up and reinforced it with cross-boards. Then we would stop by the KFC and buy a bucket of fried chicken. Pigs go crazy for fried chicken. We would back the pickup to the gate where the pig was in a field, and create a "cookie trail" of fried chicken right up the homemade ramp into the back of the pickup. We had to be careful, since big boars are mean as snakes, and it was hard to see at night. The key was getting that pig to eat the first piece of fried chicken. After that, he was hooked. The other trick was keeping the other pigs from gobbling up the chicken and running up the ramp into the back of the pickup. We wanted only one, and we wanted the biggest one.

One night, we made a successful "pigup," as we called it, so now we were flooring it to get out of this farm, and usually enough commotion has occurred that the farmer's lights were coming on and he was coming out with a shotgun to see what the heck was going on.

We headed out his farm lane with the pig in the back of the pickup. The next stop was going to be the backyard of some family who happened to have a girl in our high school class who was very stuck up and deserved a pig in her backyard.

But this one night, the farmer calls the sheriff as we are heading out of his farm lane, and the sheriff happens to be close by. We are only a few minutes out of the farm when we have sheriff lights on us, a few hills back. It is very hilly and we know we only have a few more hills before he will be pulling us over. So we quickly pull off the side of the road and the two of us hustle the big pig, using more fried chicken, into the front of the cab of the pickup. We manage to get a coat around the pig and put a baseball cap on his head and prop him up in between us. He is mighty big, so we are smashed in the cab now. We get back on the road just as the sheriff is coming over the top of the hill, descending down on us. We keep the pig happy with fried chicken as the sheriff pulls us over. The pig is sitting up between us.

The sheriff gets out of his squad car and walks up to my driver's side window. The sheriff's flashlight does not go on; he clicks it a few times, but the batteries are dead. There are no street lights. My friend is on the passenger side, the big pig wedged into the middle.

"You boys know anything about somebody stealing a prize pig?" he asks.

I look over at the pig, who is still chewing on some fried chicken, and at my friend who is now also eating a piece of fried chicken, and I look back at the sheriff and say, "No, we just went out to get some fried chicken, would you like some?" and offer him the bucket.

But that causes a major commotion from the pig, because the chicken bucket moves away from him and he tries to rock forward in his seat to get the chicken.

The sheriff says, "Don't mind if I do," and takes a piece.

Then he says, "Who are you boys?" and I say, "We're the Martin boys, I'm Ted, and these are my two brothers."

The sheriff tries to get a better look inside, but with no flashlight and no streetlights, he can't see the pig. The sheriff ponders a few minutes and then says, "You boys keep an eye out for a stolen pig, ya hear?"

I say, "Will do, sheriff," and we drive off.

Coning

Another favorite practical joke in high school was "coning." We would spend a month collecting orange construction cones from all over town and hiding them behind a shed at Rick's house. After we had fifty of them, we would go out at 2:00 a.m. and plant the cones in the road to cause traffic from both directions to end up in the driveway of someone's house, such as an attractive stuck-up girl in our class who would not give us the time of day. So, at 7:00 a.m., the coned home would end up with a huge car jam with horns blaring in their driveway. No way to back up the cars, total chaos. We only "coned" a person who deserved it, at least according to us.

Tennis Night

Doc recalled the time that he played in a round-robin tennis group in nearby Middletown in the winter on Wednesday nights on indoor courts. They counted points during the season and they had talked about trophy or prize money for the season point winner. They always had an end-of-season cocktail party for fun. One year, the guy who won the most points, Bob, was very proud of the fact that he had won the points total and was number one in the standings at the end of the season. He repeatedly asked Doc, the organizer, what he had won.

Doc said, "Come to the cocktail party tonight at Tommy's house and you'll receive your prize."

As the party progressed into the evening, Bob came up to Doc and said, "When do I get my prize?"

Doc replied, "Be patient."

Doc waited for the host to get more beer from his garage, then Doc dinged his glass with a fork and asked everyone to gather in the kitchen, where there was a TV on the kitchen counter. The host was still in the garage as Doc said, "On behalf of all the guys in the league, we pitched in to get you this TV"—and pointed to the host's TV on the kitchen counter—"because you are such a great player and finished as our points leader!"

Everyone applauded and yelled, "Way to go, Bob!"

Bob said, "Thank you, it was a lot of fun, let's do it again next year."

And the party continued. At the end of the night, Bob picked up the host's TV that he had "won" and started carrying the TV out of the house. Doc had unplugged the TV and neatly folded the cord so Bob could perceive it as a gift. The host was at the front door, ready to shake hands with everyone as they departed. Bob got to the door first as everyone else hung back. Bob said, "Thank you for hosting, I would shake your hand but my hands are full with my prize."

The host responded, "Martin must have something to do with this. Put my TV back on the kitchen counter!" as everyone else roared with laughter. The humiliated Bob was never friendly to Doc again.

Road Trip

No one ever forgets a big road trip, one where the bigger memory is the road trip itself and not the destination.

We were on one of those road trips, driving north on I-75 somewhere in Southern Georgia. I was driving Doc, now eighty-eight years old, from his Florida home to his place in Northern Michigan. Why were we driving and not flying when we could afford to fly? It was a generational thing. He needed a car up in Michigan, and he would never spend the money to fly himself up, plus pay a college kid to drive his car up there.

He thought I took a lot of vacation time, so why not have me drive him? He had also fainted on previous flights, due to his weak blood pressure and heart condition. What the heck, we might not have that many more years together, and he has been a great dad, so it's the least I can do.

So we are driving again, fourth year in a row. We always stop at the Martin Meadows in Ohio, and try to figure out what we are going to do with it one day.

"Doc, have you ever been to a Subway?" I ask, as I'm getting hungry for lunch.

I introduced him to a bagel at age 70, sushi at age 75, Mexican food at age 80. He decided he didn't care for any of them.

"I've been on a subway," he replied, "and that reminds me of the time we hijacked the trolley in Chicago."

"Do tell," I said, even though I already know the story.

Doc begins. "I was in the Marines, stationed at Navy Pier in Chicago before we shipped out to Korea. One night, we took the trolley back downtown from a party in Evanston. We had been drinking and we were all wound up. As we approached downtown's Lake Shore Drive, the trolley conductor had to stop and get out of the trolley to switch the contacts to pick up the new set of tracks. When he got out, I moved up to the driver's seat. As soon as he switched the contacts, I hit the accelerator pedal and off we zoomed toward the Outer Drive. I didn't know how to slow it, and we approached the divider that split North Lake Shore Drive from South Lake Shore Drive at the time. The hijacked trolley hit the divider and jumped up onto it, and we were stuck three feet off the ground in a sudden stop. We got out and high-tailed it for Navy Pier. It took a crane to lift the trolley off the divider the next day, and it made the newspapers. We shipped out for Korea two days later and we did not rest easy until we pulled away from the dock at Navy Pier."

We continue down the highway. "Well, Doc, your trolley story reminds me of the time we hijacked a bus."

We are now going to swap "hijack" stories.

I played water polo in college, and we were playing our archrival for the state title. They were our enemy, and it came down to the two of us every year. We had just been "homered" by the referees at their pool in the state final. "Homered" means that if we touched them, a foul was called, but meanwhile they were allowed to "mug" us with no fouls called. Turns out, the head ref was related to their coach, so we walked out of their natatorium frustrated and mad. We were walking along past the basketball arena back to the athletic dorm and their basketball bus was parked out front, ready to take the basketball team to an away game. One of us tried the door to the bus, and it opened. The keys were in the ignition. The whole water polo team hopped on, we started it up, and we drove right off campus to a very busy nearby intersection downtown; we parked the bus crossways in the intersection, blocking traffic in all four directions. Then we got off the bus and walked back to campus as car horns started blaring. It made the newspapers the next day, as they had to find a bus driver to get the bus out of the intersection.

We take an exit and pull into a Subway. "What do you want from Subway, Doc?"

"I'll have what you have." That was his standard response for trying any new food. "Okay, Doc, I'm going to have a turkey sub and load it with veggies; this is going to be healthy."

He has made it all the way to eighty-eight without ever worrying about what he eats. He never worried about the amount of red meat, and we ate a ton of steaks growing up. Big, huge Fred Flintstone-style steaks, and we never cut the fat from the steaks.

"Why would you cut off the flavor?" he used to say.

We would get excited about the steaks as we were cooking

them. We raised Black Angus beef cattle on Martin Meadows and we always put a half-steer into our own freezer each year just for our family, and we ate beef every other night: tongue sandwiches, sweetbreads, brisket, short ribs, roast beef, pot roast, beef Stroganoff, plus every cut of steak.

I get in line at Subway while Doc makes his way to the men's room. He gets back to the car first, and he is not happy that I locked the car. I can see his mouth moving and can just imagine the swear words coming out with his frustration. He never locks cars, not at the farm, not in Michigan, not in Florida. That is the privilege of growing up in rural Ohio and later living in safe areas. I hit the unlock button from where I'm standing in line in Subway. It is tough for him to get in and out of the car with bad hips, knees, ankles, and shoulders. Degenerative joint disease is tough in old age. He needs everything replaced, and he already has two artificial hips and two artificial knees.

We get in the car and start rolling again, eating while driving. Eating in the car is one of our family traditions based on the principle of saving time and money. There are too many veggies on Doc's Subway sandwich and too much mustard, and Doc quickly has a mess in his lap.

"Great sandwich idea, this thing is a disaster," says Doc.

I try to explain, "You need to keep it all tight or it unravels on you."

I should have warned him upfront.

Doc grumbles, "Now you tell me. I have a chef salad with

mustard in my lap."

He picks out the turkey and eats it, then rolls the rest of the mess back into the bag. He pours a glass of red wine from a coffee thermos and glances at his watch to make sure that it's past noon. Doc's rule is red wine with lunch, coffee after lunch. Vodka starts at 5:00 p.m.

After lunch, he wants to listen to a book on tape. I try to listen, but it's driving me crazy. The voice is just a very tough one to tolerate, especially at the volume that Doc requires to hear it. I can't even remember the book; I just need to turn it off. He agrees and we go back to telling farm stories.

I ask Doc how we ended up on our farm called Martin Meadows. Doc tells me how his side of the family was from the Alsace-Lorraine region, a combination of French and German heritage. They came to America around 1800, got a covered wagon to head west to the promising farm land of California (think *Grapes of Wrath*). They stopped for several days in Southwestern Ohio in the Great Miami River Valley, next to Dick's Creek, where the farm is today. They were intending to continue heading west to California when they encountered another family returning from California. This family warned them of no land, no jobs, and terrible dust, so the Martins homestaked the land around Dick's Creek and started making bricks from the abundant clay in the area. As kids, we all got stuck in this clay along the creek bank. They built the farmhouse, brick by brick, which still stands today. So the Martins settled on three hundred acres between what is now Middletown and Hamilton, between Dayton and Cincinnati, off Route 4. This was Shawnee country, with the center of the Shawnee Nation in nearby Chillicothe. There were Shawnee encampments along the Great Miami and Little Miami Rivers, and later the Miami Indians took over the area. If we dug on our farm, we found arrowheads, pottery shards, and Indian bones.

So the area of Butler County became heavily populated with Martin farmers. Doc grew up spending every summer working on various Martin family farms, either his own or an uncle's farm. I did the same until I figured out that most other jobs out there paid more and I could interact with peers. Farm work is lonely work, so anyone who wants to be a farmer better enjoy solitude.

The Law of Eminent Domain split our farm in half in the early nineteen-hundreds, when Route 4 Highway was constructed right through the middle of our three hundred acres. We sold off the west side of the highway, so now we had one hundred fifty acres. Later, we sold fifty acres to a neighbor.

Texas Roadhouse

We keep rolling along through Day One of our road trip. Doc is enjoying his vodka as the miles roll by. He has always liked to eat, and has lots of favorite foods.

"Why don't we get some ribs tonight?" he says excitedly.

We eventually stop at a Texas Roadhouse and order the ribs. Our waitress is a black woman, medium build with an afro. Doc looks at the menu. He looks up at me like he just found a hundred dollar bill on the sidewalk.

"Do you see what I'm seeing?" he asks.

I say, "No."

"Look at the ribs," and I look, but nothing jumps out at me.

"The half rack is $11, and the whole rack is $14, only $3 more. That makes it impossible to order the half rack," he says.

"But what if you only want a half rack?" I ask.

"Impossible," he replies. "The pricing makes it impossible to want the half rack."

This sums up his financial perspective on life. He could never allow himself to play nine holes of golf—the price was too high per hole. It didn't matter that it cost less than eighteen holes; the price/hole correlation prevented him from ever paying for nine holes. The ribs fit his same paradigm.

So we are at this restaurant with our black waitress and she brings the ribs. We start eating them, and at the first bite Doc tells me that his ribs are cold. Mine are cold as well. Doc starts looking for our waitress. An African American lady, a customer, happens to be walking down the aisle, heading back to her table. The customer is coming from the same direction as our waitress.

Before I can stop him, Doc reaches out into the aisle, grabs the woman by her arm and says, “My ribs are cold.”

This woman is not wearing anything remotely close to the waitress outfit. Same build and height, I will give him that. As I die of embarrassment, she pulls away from his grip, announces that she does not work there, and moves on, clearly rattled.

Doc looks at me in disbelief, and asks, “That’s not our waitress?”

I cannot stop shaking my head in disbelief and amusement. The irony is that I have been on the other side of this equation. My friend Ken and I were the only two white men on an all-African American not-for-profit board. We were the same height and build, but that was it. I had black hair, he had brown hair, and our faces were not similar. Yet most of the African American board members could not tell us apart. They just kept guessing at who was Ted and who was Ken at each board meeting.

Korean War Stories

As we drive along, I ask Doc about his Korean War experience. He likes to share his war stories. He tells this one:

"I took my shotgun to Korea. One day, I decided to shoot some geese, as I was sick of eating K rations. I was hiding in some marshes along the Inchon River and I shot three Egyptian geese into the river. There had been no reported enemy troop movements in the area for a few days, but I was nervous about the three shotgun blasts. I continued to scan the other side of the river after I shot them, and I waited ten minutes; all was quiet and calm, so I sprinted out through the mud flats of the river in six inches of water. I grabbed the first dead goose when a .50-caliber machine gun opened fire on me from the other bank from five hundred yards away, concealed by the cattails. I turned with the one goose and raced back for my cattails, water spray kicking up all around me from the flying bullets. I guarantee I broke the world record for the hundred-yard dash, running in army boots while carrying a goose and a shotgun. When I got close to the cattails, I dove like Pete Rose used to dive into first base and am lucky I didn't get hit. The machine gun stopped spraying as soon as they couldn't see me anymore. Pretty risky experience for a goose, but it made the goose all that much tastier!

"We later had a group of Marines pinned down on an island in the middle of the Inchon River, and we were going to rescue them at night under cover of darkness with boats. The operation was code-named 'Esther Williams,' one of the great female pin-ups during the war, because it was going to be a "wet snatch."

"The first time I heard an enemy mortar round land near me, I was smoking the stump of a cigar. I hit the deck like everyone else and afterwards, I noticed that I was no longer smoking my cigar. I had swallowed it whole when I hit the ground!

"One day I was bored, so I went with my shotgun and shot crows at the garbage dump. A Korean village boy followed me and ran out to pick up the first crow that dropped. I explained to him that I did not want to eat the crow, and that he could leave it. He smiled and pointed at himself. He wanted to take the crow home to his family to eat it! From then on I had a group of Koreans following me out to the garbage dump to take the dead crows that I shot. I am not sure where our expression "eating crow" came from, but the Koreans considered crow to be a delicacy. From then on I was known as The Great White Crow Hunter. Since they loved it, I decided to try it and found it to be horrible. It was gamey and oily, closer to raccoon than a good game bird. We had a perfect symbiotic relationship: I got to shoot away, and they got to eat them! We were perfect companions, as they had no interest in the ducks and geese that I shot, and I had no interest in the crows.

"I was on leave in Tokyo for a week, and I bought a new Japanese camera. I had it over my shoulder on its strap. I was walking down a crowded, busy street when suddenly a civilian

Korean guy came up to me, pulled out a knife and cut the camera strap from my shoulder, took my camera, and raced toward an empty alley. I took off after him, but he was fast and when I reached the alley he was twenty-five yards ahead of me. I yelled at him to stop, and when he didn't, I pulled out my .45 and fired a shot several feet over his head into the wall of a building. He froze as I walked up to him with my gun still drawn, and with his knees shaking, he handed my camera back and then took off running again. Pretty sure a soldier could not do that today and get away with it."

"In Korea, I was behind the lines and handled regular dental care, and occasionally guys who were wounded in the mouth and teeth area came to my tent. One day, I'm working on a guy and the North Koreans start shelling us, and a six-inch bomb fragment comes whizzing through the top of the tent, right between my head and my patient's head, embedding itself in my cot. I still have that fragment today. All we both heard was a quick zipper-like sound, and then a thunk. I kept right on working on his mouth. You have to be lucky in life.

"I was able to bring my .45 and a Chinese army rifle back from the war. The rifle the North Koreans used was made in Russia and was fired at us by the Chinese. That war was definitely a proxy war between Communism and democracy, with Russia and China both supporting the North Korean invasion of South Korea with troops, arms, equipment, supplies, and MIGs."

Restaurant Stop

We continue on Day Two of our road trip. As we drive into some hilly areas of Tennessee, we see a sign on the side of the highway for "Falling Rock." It reminds me that I named my high school band *Falling Rock* so that we would get free advertising on all the roads that were cut through the cliffs across the country.

We are tired of driving, so we decide to stop for dinner at a restaurant where we can get a drink. Doc always drank vodka on the rocks, for as long as I can remember. One of his favorite lines at the farm was to offer someone a Bloody Mary if it was before noon. The guest would say, "Sure," and then Doc would pour two glasses of vodka on the rocks, one for him and one for the guest. "Here's your Bloody Mary. Sorry, I just ran out of both Bloody and Mary, but it's still a great drink."

We pick a restaurant that looks like they serve hard liquor. As soon as we sit down, Doc looks for a waiter. A water boy approaches to pour water.

"I'll have a vodka on the rocks," says Doc.

I see this coming a mile away.

"He only does water," I say.

The water boy does not even look up; he pours two waters and moves on.

Doc looks at me in frustration.

"He can't take a vodka order?" asks Doc.

"No, the waiter does that."

"I am not tipping the water boy," says Doc.

The waiter arrives, and he's clearly "light in the loafers," as Doc would say. It took Doc up to age seventy to understand what a homosexual actually is, and he was flabbergasted by the realization. Doc immediately starts raising his eyebrows and making "sweetheart" faces at me as the waiter goes into his full routine, with extra "flair." Doc orders slowly and loudly. He must assume gays have trouble hearing and understanding English, just like he talks to anyone who has a slight foreign accent. Doc wants a vodka on ice, and to fill it up, he wants a decent pour, but he does it with mock feminine style, complete with hand flourish and gestures. I know the waiter sees right through this. As he leaves with the drink order, I explain to Doc that he cannot continue with the mimicking. I believe this is going to go badly.

When the waiter comes back with the drink he says to Doc, "Were you making fun of me?"

Doc says, "Oh, no, some of my best friends are just like you."

And the waiter then says, "Okay, then I will give you your drink."

He sets down the drink in front of Doc, and the drink is full to the brim with vodka. Doc now thinks he is being charged for two drinks.

"Is this a single drink charge?" Doc asks.

The waiter says, "Yes, it is."

Doc beams a big grin and looks at me and says, "I love this boy!"

To which the waiter and I explode in laughter. Doc has completely defused the uncomfortable dialogue with just the right humor angle. He has been able to do that his whole life—get in trouble, but get back out with humor.

The waiter reminds Doc of a surgeon in our town named Wayne who also had effeminate mannerisms. The surgeon almost tiptoed when he walked, and Doc was always amused by his flowery hand gestures and flamboyant style. When our bull was young, it developed an infection in its hooves, so the bull began to "tip-toe" on its hooves because of the pain. As a result, Doc named the bull "Wayne."

My parents liked to host a Kentucky Derby party at Martin Meadows. They would set up a TV in the barn on the hay bales, so everyone could be outside drinking Mint Juleps as the sun set. I was almost eleven years old and came flying around the corner of the barn into the party, shouting, "Dad, Wayne just got out!"

Doctor Wayne happened to be at this party, and he said to me, "You have a cow named Wayne?"

I said, "Yes, he is our bull who walks just like you," and the party roared as Doctor Wayne turned bright red.

Back on the Farm

Our key stopover on this road trip from Florida is our farm outside Middletown, Ohio. We pull in at about 5:00 p.m. at the end of Day Three, just in time for a cold beer. We always stop at the farm to check on it, because we need to feel it again.

We have a guy living there, Pat, a good local guy. Pat stopped paying rent years ago, but he doesn't steal from us. In this area, it's tough to find someone who won't steal from you, so we let the rent issue go.

Pat set up a pool table under the outside porch, so the three of us start enjoying the evening with some cold beer and "cutthroat," the three-way pool game we have played forever. Doc always plays for a quarter per person, per game. Doc has very colorful pool table language that he invented himself. He calls the corners on each side of any pocket the "lop ears." So if I am about to take a shot at a pocket, and there is the slightest bit of angle involved, he will point to a corner and say, "Careful of the lop-ear on this shot, it's gonna be tough to avoid." If I make a shot but my cue ball ends up in a poor position for my next shot, he would state, "You just sewed your own ass." If he makes a great shot, he lets out a "Mitt ougen!" yell, which is "with eyes" in German, meaning he made a great deadeye shot. If I have to make a long shot, he shakes his head in pity and says, "Too much green. Arnie Palmer couldn't make a golf ball go straight for that far." If we are playing doubles, and he wants me to hit it softly, he says, "Coozey it up." If he wants me to hit it hard, he says, "Put a Rap-a-Cock on it." If he drills a shot with velocity, he exclaims, "Rap-a-Cock Home!"

It gets late, and Doc goes to bed. Pat changes the stakes to a dollar per game. I have soon lost all my dollars, as Pat is a very good pool player. I don't want to go to the car and get my wallet, since I will end up with no money left. So I tell Pat I'm all out of dollar bills.

"Then we need to play for June bugs," he says.

"What?" I say.

"Whoever loses each game, that person needs to eat a June bug that the other person hands him."

"Fine," I say. I'm tired of losing money and have never eaten a June bug. June bugs are buzzing and humming all over the place, go figure, as it happens to be the first week of June. I lose the next game and Pat carefully hunts for a big, juicy, very active and buzzing June bug.

"Here you go," he says, and hands me the captured bug.

They have a pretty stout back end, which could be full of nasty bug juice. I decide my best method is to wash it down with beer and avoid crunching it in my mouth. The problem is that Mr. June Bug decides it does not want to get washed down my throat, so he unfolds his wings and digs in to my throat with his claws just as I almost have him down the gullet. Reminds me of Don Gullet, '72 Reds. So I exhale an explosion of beer and June bug all over the porch, much to the roaring laughter of Pat.

"That's the reason we play for June bugs, the entertainment factor," he guffaws.

"If you crunch them open, it's too nasty to stomach. If you try and swallow them whole, they spread their wings and grab onto your throat," as tears of laugher roll down his face.

It's 1:00 a.m., I have had too many beers, and Pat is suggesting we head into the Moose Lodge. Nothing ever good happens at that time of night, especially if a car is involved. Even eating that late is a bad idea. First, you'll eat something you normally wouldn't want, second, you'll eat too much of it, and third, you'll feel horrible in the morning. So I pass on the Moose Lodge trip and head up to find a bed.

Pat has moved his family members into the upstairs of the farmhouse. What I don't know is that his sister has adopted several of the stray barn cats as house pets, and there are now lots of cats sleeping upstairs each night. I go into my old room. I take off my coat and drop it on the floor (huge mistake), and go to sleep. In the morning, two cats have slept on my coat and both pissed on it during the night. They must have smelled my dogs on the jacket, so they marked their territory. I can still smell cat piss on my jacket even after multiple washings and dry cleanings.

The next day, we are rummaging around collecting stuff to take out of the farmhouse. I open a closet and see my old Stetson from high school. It's lying on its top to protect the brim, up in the shelf above the hangars. Without bothering to look into the hat, I reach up and grab it and place it on my head. I'm immediately hollering and jumping around, and have to throw the hat off my head. A family of mice was nesting in the hat, and I just dumped the whole family into my hair with the hat trapping them on top of my head. My hair was crawling with frantic mice, a horrible feeling. I scrape them all off my head and they go scurrying in all directions as they hit the floor.

Doc would hang an old straw cowboy hat out on the front porch in the winter, and sparrows would always build a nest in the hat, with the opening facing the wall. When we had guests over, he would go over to the hat and say, "Let's go to the barn, I will get my hat." Then he would put it on his head and quickly lift it off, as several young sparrows would go flying out. It looked like the best magic trick ever.

The Meadows

The next night at the farm, we head to the only good restaurant in town, called The Meadows. This is where Speaker of the House John Boehner always came to dinner when he was in town. Doc knows the waiters and they greet him as we walk in. He badly wants to be recognized by someone in the restaurant. Most people need to feel wanted, not just by family members but also by a community. He searches the room for a familiar face, but does not see one. He sees his bartender friend making a drink, and the bartender says, "Hello, Ted."

Doc smiles at me and says, "Look, he's making my drink for me without me ordering, he remembers!"

I doubt it, but I let it pass as the drink gets delivered to another table. I can see that it is a bad idea to set yourself up for little emotional letdowns.

I remember Doc doing the same thing when the Keeley Dental Society of Cincinnati called to convince him to attend their annual meeting.

"Hey, they must be honoring me," he thought, and he worked on an acceptance speech for two days. He went, but he did not receive an award, they were simply drumming up attendance. Try not to make assumptions, that's one of life's best lessons. But Doc turns around and goes up as quick as he goes down, and we have a fun dinner, telling farm stories. He has the ability to immediately bounce back from disappointments, both small and large. He can shrug it off and laugh about it five minutes later. And he always hits the reset button the next day, no matter what happens. Keep rolling forward and don't look back, that's how he rolls.

"Life happens through the front windshield, not the rear view mirror," he likes to say.

Deaf Preacher

Doc's father, Grandpa Martin, was a foreman at Armco Steel Corporation. When they poured the slag, the molten sparks flew everywhere and burned through clothes and into the worker's skin. So he had all these little burn marks all over him. He would work the farm in the early morning and evenings, and work at the mill all day. He did not seem to have much of a sense of humor.

Back then, the preacher of the church traveled around to each farm and stayed with each family for a week. Grandpa did not think much of this preacher tradition because he felt like it was a freeloading practice to get free meals, plus it required listening to the preacher reading from the Bible after each meal. Grandpa would be up at 5:00 a.m. and would have already tended to the cows before breakfast. He would come in cold, tired, and hungry, just as the preacher rolled down the steps for breakfast in his bathrobe. Then the preacher would delay everyone after breakfast with prayers, preventing Grandpa from getting to work on time. This really started to wear on Grandpa, who was already short-tempered by nature.

Grandpa's philosophy was that he would occasionally go to church to pray, but he would never think of bringing the church back to his house. He resented the preacher and disliked the custom. This minister was also nearly deaf, so it made for some real tension. At one particular dinner, Grandpa was fed up with the preacher being at our farm for too long. He asked the preacher to "please pass the potatoes."

The preacher didn't hear him, as he forgot to put in his hearing aid for dinner.

Grandpa said it louder this time, and I could see his temper rising. I knew this was going to go badly unless the preacher passed the potatoes quickly.

"Preacher Jones, pass those potatoes," a third request, no longer with a friendly tone. The preacher did not hear him.

My mother reached over to tap the preacher's arm to try and save him, but it was too late. At this point, Grandpa took a hard roll from his plate and threw it as hard as he could the length of the table and beaned the preacher square in the forehead. Then Grandpa yelled, "Tell that deaf son-of-a-bitch to pass the potatoes!"

The preacher passed the potatoes, and he never came back to stay at Martin Meadows again.

Driving with Grandpa

Doc tried to give me a buzz haircut with the cattle shears one summer, and he accidentally put a gash in the side of my head that required several stitches. While I was no longer being cattle sheared, I was now being sent with Grandpa for every haircut. Grandpa, now in his eighties, would pick me up in his 1952 Rambler station wagon, which felt like a bag of bolts that would break apart at anything over twenty mph. I'm not sure whose idea it was that Grandpa should take me for haircuts, but I thought I was going to die on every trip. He was a terrible driver, one of those drivers who never quite turns the wheel far enough, notices the turn too late, and must over-brake or be forced to go careening into the turn.

He took me to his barber, a friend of his who must have been ninety years old, and of course, he couldn't see well. The barber was also hard of hearing, so it didn't matter what I said about how I wanted my hair cut. He cut it the only way he knew how, which was a buzz-cut with a half-inch of hair left in the front that he would stick straight up with pink sticky stuff that felt and smelled like bubblegum. I had outgrown that haircut, never liked it, and still didn't want it. It did not matter; that is what I got. Then there was the death ride home. By the seventh grade, the haircut was too embarrassing and I simply disappeared in the woods one day when Grandpa came to pick me up.

His driving continued to go downhill, and one night he

pulled into our driveway with a sheriff's car following him. Grandpa came shuffling into the house, followed by the sheriff. I couldn't wait to hear this one. Grandpa headed around the corner to hide, and Doc asked the sheriff, "Is there a problem, officer?"

"He was driving eighty miles an hour on I-75," said the exasperated officer, who seemed to be highly stressed and soaked in sweat.

"That's only five miles over the speed limit," said Doc.

"He was doing eighty going the wrong way!" said the shaking officer.

And that was the end of Grandpa's driver's license. No one got killed, and according to the government, he was off the road. But he just kept driving without a license, and no one could take his car keys away.

Not long after that, Grandpa was in the hospital after a car wreck into a tree, and he had a broken ribcage and a broken jaw. He could not really speak.

A nurse came in and asked if he needed anything. He wanted to know whether his test results were back. Through the wired jaw he tried to ask, "Har my testrers black?"

She thought she understood him. She folded back his top sheet, and leaned over the bed to take a closer look. She lifted up his hospital gown and bent down over his crotch. She put the gown back down and said to him, "No, your testicles are not black."

Grandpa shook his head, took out a sheet of paper, and wrote, “Are my test results back?”

The nurse read it, turned bright red, and walked out of the room.

Doc later went to visit Grandpa in the hospital, but he had not been in to visit him for over a week, too long in Grandpa’s mind. He walked into his hospital room and sat down on a chair, but Grandpa motioned him to come closer and used a hoarse whisper to say, “Gotta tell you something, come close.”

Doc leaned over the hospital bed and put his ear close to Grandpa’s mouth, and suddenly Grandpa sucker-punched him in the face!

Doc reeled backward holding his nose, and exclaimed, “What the Sam Hell was that for?”

And Grandpa said, “That was for not coming to see me for a week. Now have a seat and let’s talk.”

The Pastures Open

Doc and I designed a nine-hole golf course that meandered across Martin Meadows. We drove metal fenceposts into the ground for the pins and tied flags around each post. Each golfer carried a ten-foot string with a small metal loop on one end. There was no putting; the golfer had to hit the ball within the ten-foot diameter circle for it to be "in the hole." The golfer put the loop over the flag pin post and pulled the string out to make sure the golf ball was inside the ten-foot circumference. It looked a lot like stretching the chains in a football game to see if it was a first down. Instead of a first down, the players were in the hole. Golfers had to play the ball wherever it landed on the farm, no matter what, so no "unplayable lie" existed. If the ball landed in a cow paddy, it had to be hit out of the cow paddy. If the ball was in a multi-floral rose bush, the golfer had to hack his way out and get bloodied from the thorns. We had lots of holes where players had to hit the tee shot into a field full of cattle. Hitting a cow was a one-stroke penalty, hitting a calf was a two-stroke penalty. The cows would jump from being startled by a golf ball landing near them. But if it wasn't Doc or me hitting the shot, we would simultaneously yell, "two-stroke penalty" as soon as a cow or calf jumped, whether they were hit or not. But if he or I hit one, we would support each other's claims that it was a "startlement flinch" and not an actual "hit." We hung a brown jacket behind the manure spreader and splattered it with manure.

Then, after the round, we would have an awards ceremony just like the Masters, except it was for the "Pastures", and the previous year's winner would put the coveted brown jacket on this year's winner, with all the same pomp and circumstance as the Masters.

We traveled the course with a pickup truck, which held all the golf bags, the beer cooler, and the tee box markers. The tee markers were Kamchatka Vodka bottles filled with water and painted with the hole number on the side of the bottles in red fingernail polish. As we played each hole, we picked up the bottles so the cows didn't step on them and crush the glass bottles. The cows liked to rub against the golf pin stakes to scratch, so they were usually leaning over. The pins usually had cows around each one, so the approach shot had to be planned carefully to avoid a penalty. A couple from Cincinnati came up, two good friends from high school who married each other. They both loved The Pastures Open and they never missed it. Our foursome was Doc and me against Will and Paula, and we were all tied going into the ninth hole. Cows surrounded the ninth hole pin, so anyone shooting at the pin was going to risk a two-stroke penalty. Plus, the pin was tucked tightly into a half-circle of multi-floral rose bushes. There was risk of bouncing the golf ball off the side of a cow into the bushes. Doc and I chose to lay-up outside the trouble; we hit short versus risk a cow flinch or ball in the rose bushes.

After we both hit, the cows start moving and they opened

up a clear shot to the hole. Will told Paula to go for the pin. She hit too much club and the ball soared over the pin into a group of cows, and we clearly saw one flinch.

"Two-stroke penalty," we exclaimed.

But Will knocked one stiff twelve feet from the pin, so we know he is going to chip in for a two.

Doc successfully hit his chip inside the ten-foot ring for his two. My ball was buried deep in a cow paddy and it took me one blast to extricate it, then another to chip in, for a three. Paula must find her ball and chip in to beat my three, as we were playing best ball of two, with the high ball breaking the tie. If she couldn't find her ball, her best score was a four and we would win the front nine. Will and Paula were looking for her ball but couldn't find it. Will then noticed that a cow had a golf ball halfway wedged into its behind. He knew Paula played a Titleist 2; he got up close to the back of the cow, lifted up the tail, turned to Paula and said, "This looks like yours!" but she couldn't see the ball from the side angle and she thought Will was poking fun at her increasing butt size, so she came over and swung her golf club at his leg and hit him in the knee, dropping him.

Doc and I were howling at the situation, plus we needed to make up a rule for the one scenario we never envisioned happening at the Pastures Open.

Doc said, "Ball wedged in cow's behind, one-stroke penalty for hitting the cow, plus one-stroke penalty for inability to strike your ball."

Then he added, "Striking your partner with golf club, another two-stroke penalty. Paula has a 4, Ted has a 3, high ball breaks the tie, and we win the front nine."

Rhea Herd

We raised Black Angus on Martin Meadows for over fifty years, and cattle break down fences non-stop. Doc was getting too old to repair them. Cows think the grass always looks greener on the other side, so they press their thousand-pound bodies against the fence and lean their necks, breaking the strongest fence over time. The other theory is that cattle test the outside perimeter by leaning against the fence to make sure they are safe. Only after they believe they are safe from predators will they eat the grass in the middle of the field. And that is why they constantly break down the fences. I say, "Bull" to the perimeter-testing theory. The grass looks greener on the other side, and humans think the same way. On a cattle farm, you spend half your time picking up sticks and fixing fences. You pick up all the sticks so you don't break a blade on your bush-hog. You fix the fences so your cows do not escape. Doc is tired of mowing and fixing fences.

Now the ostrich craze is red-hot in restaurants, and Doc's wheels are turning. What Doc really needs is something new to entertain him, and restaurants are all serving ostrich as the new great low-cholesterol white meat. My Uncle Fred leads the way and buys two ostriches. We go over to see them, and the first thing we notice are the nine-foot fences required to hold in the ostriches. Clearly more work than cattle. As we ask Uncle Fred about them, the two ostriches start hissing at us through the fence. Then the male drops to his knees and starts swinging his wings like signal flags, alternating each one in a crazy mating ritual dance.

Uncle Fred declares that the male has locked in on Doc and clearly wants to have his way with him. We laugh hysterically and at the same time, speculate that ostriches might be more than we could handle. Uncle Fred says he should have bought rheas. We have never heard of them. He explains that there are three versions of ratites—three-toed birds that have wings but cannot fly: ostrich, emu, and rhea. The rhea is the smallest of the three. Ninety percent of all restaurant meat listed as ostrich is actually rhea meat, since they are easier to raise and no one knows the difference between ostrich, emu, and rhea meat. Uncle Fred goes on to say that ostriches are too dangerous to raise, they can kill you with one big beak peck. But he has heard of some local farmers doing really well with rheas. And, he says, southern Ohio has the same topography and climate as the pampas grassland of Argentina.

Not stopping to think about the fact that Argentina is four thousand miles south of Middletown, Ohio, we get "rhea fever." We want in on "ratite gold," time to strike and take advantage of the restaurant craze. So we buy twenty-eight rhea chicks and await their arrival. It is a fifty-fifty joint venture for Doc and me; they cost about $2,000 each. So for roughly $30,000 each, we are about to make a fortune in the rhea business!

I'm living and working in Chicago, so I miss the rhea

delivery. Doc explains they seem to be thriving and growing well. We are going to set up a breeder operation, just like with cattle, and we will sell off the next generation of chicks to other farmers to get them into the rhea business, unless we are going to make more by selling directly to the restaurant operating companies. We know that the rhea meat price is twice what farmers are getting for beef, and Doc is reinvigorated by having a new project. The first three months go according to plan. They eat and grow, simple as that.

I plan a trip with the family to visit our rhea herd. We bring everyone, four kids and two Siberian Huskies. We pull up to the farmhouse and look out at a scene straight out of Jurassic Park with crazy-looking birds, five feet tall, running fast across a field. I let everyone out of the car, including the two dogs. Klondike, the six-year-old Siberian male, takes one look at twenty-eight big birds running hard across a field and his primordial instincts take over. He takes off at a dead run toward the six-foot rhea fence. In disbelief, I watch him do a Rin-Tin-Tin and launch himself over the top of the barbed wire fence. He clears it like a deer. He takes off after the nearest rhea, as all of them are now in a complete panic state, running at thirty miles an hour. Klondike tackles the nearest one and takes it down. I'm running and screaming at Klondike but am slowed by climbing the fence as he shakes the neck of the rhea. I get to his collar and pull him off the now-dead rhea. I take him out of the rhea field by the gate and Doc is there with his famous breast-pocket notepad.

"You have been here less than five minutes and you are down two thousand dollars," he says, annotating the event in his little pad.

"How do you know that was my rhea?" I ask.

"Well," he says, "Your dog just killed one of your rheas. In fact, two others have died from coyotes, and they were yours too."

"No way," I say, "We said we would split the losses fifty-fifty."

"No, no, we split up the herd and it's just bad luck that all three that have died thus far were yours!" he laughs.

He gave me advice a long time ago to stay away from any investment where it is tough to identify which ones are mine, because, as an outside investor, "mine" will always be the one that died, be it horses, cows, dogs, or ostriches.

So the next day, we are going to round up our rheas for the first time and put tags on each of their ankles. We go out in the field and approach them like we would round up cows. Our goal is to just slowly start to group them and head them toward the barn. But they want no part of it. They quickly out-maneuver us and start to move pretty fast.

Doc says, "Well, let's just get one at a time."

"Okay," I say. So we corner one and it suddenly leaps toward Doc and strikes his nose with a powerful beak peck.

Doc is down on the ground, holding his bloody nose.

"*Cripe* that hurt," says Doc as he gets up. "That felt like I just got hit by Rocky Marciano."

We retreat to the farmhouse and get on the phone with the breeder. We learn that they strike the closest thing coming at them, which means your nose if you are walking toward them. But if you can grab 'em by the neck under the chin, they will walk with you and not attack; somehow, it's like grabbing them by the balls. We head into the local sporting goods store and buy two football helmets with big face cages, and two XL first baseman mitts.

We get back to the field, helmets on, extending our mitts straight out toward the rheas as we approach them. Bam! The rhea hits the mitt with his beak and before he can get his head out of the mitt, I grab him right under the chin by the throat. He is not moving, just like the breeder said. I start walking toward the barn with him, hand clamped on his neck, and he walks right along with me.

"I got one, it works!" I yelled. I look behind me and Doc somehow has two of them, each by the neck, and he is walking them both back to the barn.

"We are back in business!" says Doc.

Unfortunately, the venture didn't pan out, due to coyote losses. The coyotes started racing up and down the fences at night, creating a panicked frenzy among the rheas all night long. The rheas stopped mating and then no more baby rheas. We solved the coyote problem with a coyote hunter, but the next spring was a very rainy one, and the new rhea chicks could not walk in the mud during spring. So they became weak and died off, one by one. So much for being like the pampas grassland of Argentina; they do not get stuck in the mud in Argentina in the spring.

ATV

Farmers like to buy vehicles. Maybe because they need so many anyway, like a tractor, combine, pickup, etc., that they just keep buying. The big tractor was for the real work of pulling a hay combine. The second, smaller tractor was for bush hogging (mowing the fields) and fixing fences with the utility wagon. It was a hassle to switch from Bush Hog to small wagon, so Doc bought an ATV to pull around the utility wagon.

One Thanksgiving, while I was still in business school, my fiancée Pam, two friends from Kellogg, Hambone and Alice, and I road-tripped from Chicago to Martin Meadows. Ham and I set up a racecourse time trial in the rain for an ATV competition (sorry you lost, Hambone). We had to drive down the big hill, around the pond, and back up the hill. Plenty of sharp turns and rapid braking was included in rain-soaked long grass. We didn't know it, but we were completely burning out the brakes on the ATV. We were using the brakes to drift around the downhill turns in the wet grass. When we were done, we hooked the ATV back up to the utility wagon.

The next day, Doc heads down to the pond area to fix some fence. He parks the ATV next to the broken fence, which is above the pond on a slight hill. He puts on the brakes and steps off. He grabs tools from the wagon and walks to the fence. He turns, as he hears movement. He watches in dismay as the ATV/wagon combo rolls in reverse down the hill right into the pond and sinks, disappearing from sight. He walks back to the farmhouse, calls me in Chicago and asks, "Any chance you burnt the brakes out on the ATV?" he asks.

"Oh shoot," I say, "what happened?"

"You owe me a new ATV and utility wagon, plus all the tools," he says.

"You mean I owe you new brakes for the ATV?" I say with hope.

"Nope," he says, and tells me what happened.

"You owe me the whole enchilada," he says, none too happy with the matter. "I will use your rheas as credit and let you know if you still own any rheas after my calculations."

"Fine," I say, since I already see ostrich meat disappearing from menus in Chicago at a rapid pace. This was my second big expense involving a vehicle. The first was the van that went into Lake Michigan.

Sunken Van

During my junior summer of college, while working in northern Michigan, my sister Jill and I got excited about a Doobie Brothers concert nearby. I took out the seats in the family van and transported eight college kids to the concert at nearby Castle Farms, Michigan. Naturally, we had to put a keg in the back of the van. The concert ended, and we had all been drinking heavily. We decided to take the Ironton Ferry to cut across Lake Charlevoix to avoid the traffic that will be crawling to Petoskey. I drove out to the end of the ferry dock and the gates were closed. It was midnight, and the sign read, "Hours: 9 a.m. - 11 p.m." The ferry closed an hour ago. The dock is twenty yards long and eight feet wide. It was pitch dark and there are no lights on the dock. I didn't want to risk driving all the way in reverse when I couldn't see out the back of the van.

So I decided to turn around on the narrow dock.

There was a big drop and jolt, a loud scraping noise, but the music was cranking in the van. The front of the van was still on the dock, sitting on the front fender. The back of the van was on the bottom of Lake Michigan, in two feet of water. I was looking up at the sky, due to my angle in the front driver seat. The guy in the passenger seat was asleep. The music was so loud that no one else was aware of what was going on. I hit the gas, and the snapped drive train under the van rotated around, splashing water from the air vents into the front of the van. Not a good sign. I opened my door, and I was at a steep angle. I looked at what I thought was a concrete parking lot, and took a hop down. It was the dead flat water of Lake Michigan. Because I thought I was going to land on asphalt, I completely lost my balance as my feet go two feet below the surface of the water and hit the sand bottom. I fell over and was completely soaked. I stood up in disbelief, but I now understood that I must have backed off the dock. I opened the sliding side van door, and the angle was way too steep. The door had too much weight and too much momentum at this angle, so I couldn't hold onto it. The door accelerated hard down the side of the van and hit the end and snapped the hinge. It did not fall off, but was permanently jammed open. Once again, not good. Now my friends started to spill out into Lake Michigan. I never turned the music off, so the radio was still blasting, thus no one could hear me when I yelled to watch their step. It was too dark to see that it was clearly a lake, so everyone did what I did: they hopped down and it resulted in a big lake flop. Everyone was soaked from head to foot, including my younger sister Mol, who landed, fell over, got up and headed the wrong way in the lake, into deeper water. I needed to run, swim and grab her arm to head her toward land.

We finally got everyone on shore and contemplated how to get the van off its perch. Suddenly, there were headlights on the dock, and along came the Doobie Brothers equipment truck, a big 18-wheeler, clearly lost.

I walk up to the window of the driver truck cab and asked, “How ‘bout a hand?”

“For what?” he inquired.

“That van of mine needs to be dragged off the dock by the rear axle, and the front bumper is about to drop into the water, then you can pull the van up the beach.”

“Not unless you pay me,” said the driver.

I went back to the group and we had $32 among us. “That’s all we have,” I said.

“That’s not enough,” said the Doobie driver.

“Your concert stunk,” I said flatly, “and we paid $18 a ticket. How about you finish our keg of beer for your trouble?”

He smiled and says, “The concert did suck. I’ll help you with one pull and then fill up my thermos with your keg beer.”

We took the chains, and I wrapped one end of the chain around the rear bumper, which was underwater. The front bumper was still stuck up on the dock.

He backed the rig up and tightened the chain, and as he started to pull tight, the entire van was pulled off the dock and came crashing down into two feet of water. He started to slowly pull the van backward, out of the water and up onto the beach, when suddenly a very loud noise erupted as the 18-wheeler ripped the back bumper off the van.

I unhooked the chain, bummed that the van damage continued to grow. I reattached the chains under the van and he pulled the van the rest of the way up the beach.

We all needed rides home, and luckily there was a pay phone in the park. I had one more bad idea, and that was to call the local tow truck man who also happened to put docks in and out of Walloon Lake over the summer, plus do garbage pick-up. He was a Canadian Indian. I went to the payphone on the beach and found his home number in the phone book. Someone answered the phone, and I said, "Hi, this is Ted Martin, can you come tow me? I'm at the Ironton Ferry Beach and need to get my dad's van back home tonight."

There was a long pause, and then he said, "If you ever call me at two a.m. again, I will slit your throat," and hung up.

I turned to the group and said, "You no call Canuck at two a.m.!"

We started to call buddies (Imbo, Dutch, Doobs) for rides home. Meanwhile, every parent was calling our house, asking where his or her child was. And by the time we got home, it was 4 a.m. I walked in, soaked from the waist down. My dad appeared from his bedroom and said, "Where the hell have you been? Every parent has been calling all night!"

"I have good news and bad news," I said.

"Give me the good news," he said.

I said, "The van is no longer in Lake Michigan."

"Go to bed," he said, and turned and walked back into his bedroom.

It took all of my summer wages to pay off the van damage.

Molly's Finger

Sister Molly and Granny were home alone. Ten-year-old Mol was trying to carry something into the farmhouse when the door slammed and her pinky finger was severed in the door. She knew Granny never had a driver's license, so she got on her bike and rode ten miles to the hospital. When she got there, the doctor saw that it was a clean cut, missing the top segment.

"Where is the end of your finger? We can sew it back on if you have it." asked the doctor.

Mol said, "It must be back in the door jam."

So they jumped in an ambulance and zoomed out to the farmhouse. When they arrived, they saw Granny cleaning up the blood around the door jam.

The doctor asked, "Where is the tip of the finger?"

Granny, not being able to see so well, replied, "Oh, there was a bloody mess that I threw into the bushes."

They started searching the bushes, when a squirrel starts chattering from the nearby birdfeeder in a tree. They look up and realize that the squirrel has Mol's fingertip in it's paws, and the squirrel is chewing on the fingertip.

"Get a rifle," the doctor says to Mol.

Mol retrieves a .22 rifle, and the doctor takes aim. He fires, and accidentally shoots the fingertip out of the squirrel's paws, instead of hitting the squirrel. It is gone. So Mol has a stumpy pinky to this day.

Talking Crow

We collected all kinds of live animals on the farm, including many wild birds. We had hawks, owls, and crows in cages, and we would always try to train them. Doc had a pair of sparrowhawks that would come back to him if he let them out to hunt. We shot starlings with a pellet gun to feed the captured raptor birds.

One day, Doc wounded a starling and it flew over my mom's laundry hanging on the clothesline, dripping a line of red blood on all of the white bed sheets. My mom was really upset about Doc ruining the white bed sheets with starling blood. Bird blood did not come out in the laundry back then.

Doc would occasionally wound a crow and then keep it in a cage and try to teach it to talk. There was a famous old hillbilly rumor that a crow was like a backwoods parrot, and my Uncle Fred had a crow that could say twenty words, so we knew it could be done. But Uncle Fred warned us that only one in every ten crows had the ability to talk and learn words, and the crow's tongue had to be split to enable human speech. We named them all "Inky," since they were all black as ink. We finally got one to say a word, but the word sounded like "crap."

I laugh at the memory of me bringing one of the crows into class for Show and Tell in the fourth grade. Everyone was surprised that we were keeping a crow in captivity, but then the crow started cawing, "Crap! Crap! Crap! Crap!" and all the kids roared with laughter.

To the teacher's horror, I was the star of Show and Tell, thanks to my swearing crow.

Elk Hunt

When I was in junior high school, Doc and I took two weeks to go hunt out west in the Bob Marshall Wilderness in Montana with Uncle "Bull" and his son "Calf," Bull's son's nickname. Uncle Bull had five horses for us and acted as our guide. He always brought an extra horse to carry supplies. Bull knew the mountains, and we spent the first two days packing in, traveling higher up in the mountains each day. Then we set up our camp for the remainder of the two weeks. Sometimes we would take the horses from camp; other times, we would tether the horses in a meadow and hike up. I was hiking a peak alone on the fourth morning when I stopped to rest. I was scanning 360° with my binoculars when I froze in my track, spotting a big bull elk down below in a meadow. I quickly took aim, heart pounding. BAM! I dropped the elk! I let out a whoop and started the hour's hike down to the meadow where my big bull should have been dead. Typically everyone else convened in the direction of a shot, which meant Doc, Bull, and Calf would be on the way.

I got to the meadow and immediately saw our tethered horses and thought, "My elk was in the meadow with our horses?"

Then a sickening feeling crept from my stomach to my head as I turned to where my elk lay dead. In the excitement of my first elk hunt, I had mistaken Bull's big brown horse for an elk. Its head had been partially blocked by dead branches, giving me the illusion of antlers through the scope.

As others arrived, Bull broke the silence by saying, "Well, the good news is you made a great shot, you dropped him stone dead with one shot right through the heart."

After I sobbed my apologies, Bull again helped the situation by explaining, "Now we can get a grizzly!"

We set up a grizzly hunt around the dead horse and waited. At dusk, a big grizzly came to feed on the horse and Doc shot him. We then cut off the grizzly hide and head and packed it onto the extra horse, which was no longer extra. Bull, Doc, and Calf rode ahead while I walked and led the packed horse with the grizzly skin and head bundled on top of the horse. The problem was that a paw came untied and flopped down onto the side of the horse, and the horse went berserk. I lost the reins as the horse reared up on its hind legs, then took off at a full gallop into the pitch-black night up the trail.

"Shit," said Bull, "Now we are down two horses!"

When we got back to camp hours later, that same horse that took off into the pitch-black night was standing there next to our tent. What a homing instinct!

Another year, we were antelope hunting in Montana with Uncle Bull. We had a good week of hunting, and we were scheduled to fly out the next day. We got a call from the meat processor, where we had taken our two deer and two antelope. Doc and Uncle Bull had attached ten-year-old licenses as tags. They never thought we would shoot more than their two licenses, meaning Bull and Doc never thought that Bull's son "Calf" and I would actually both shoot an antelope. So one of the tags read, "1968 Black Bear, Helen Lane" (Helen Lane was Uncle Bull's wife) and it was supposed to read, "1971 Antelope, Ted Martin." The processor called and said, "You put the wrong tag on this antelope, come put on the right tag. I got a game warden who comes by all the time." So the only other tag we had that was a legal current tag said, "Helen Lane, Antelope, 1971." It was the right year, right animal, but Helen Lane was a female and we were all males. So they had me wait in the car in a hooded sweatshirt pulled down low over my head. They went in to the processor's and handed him the license.

"Where is she?" the processor asked.

"She's out in the car, she's got pneumonia," said Doc.

The processor looked out the window at me in the car, and he'd seen this movie before. I tried to look as sickly as possible, hunched over in the front seat, fake coughing, not showing my face. My window was rolled down, so I could hear how it's going.

Doc yelled, "Wave from the car, Helen."

For some reason, I tried to make my hand look small and feminine, and the result was that I tucked my thumb inside the palm, put all the fingers together, and now it looked like I was waving with a hand that had no thumb and the fingers were fused together.

"What's wrong with her hand?" asked the processor.

“Fingers were fused together at birth,” said Doc, going in deeper by the minute.

“Then how did she pull the trigger?” asked the processer.

“She’s left-handed, which is her normal hand,” said Doc.

So keeping my head down still, I now turned and waved with a fully spread-out left hand, as if someone asked me to show the number five using my left hand. The processor shook his head with a look of amusement on his face.

“Our rates went up today. It now costs $100 per antelope instead of $50,” he said.

Doc and Bull practically raced for their wallets to pay the additional fee, giddy with relief that they were not being turned in to the sheriff for not having the proper license. Doc and Bull got drunk on vodka to celebrate their great escape from being too cheap to buy enough licenses for the trip. They called me Helen Lane all night, cracking up every time they said it.

We laughed about the fact that Doc once pulled out frozen antelope from our freezer that we shot in 1975. He always marked the year on the outside of a meat package. It was now 1986, so he took a magic marker and changed the 7 to an 8, so now the meat was only one year old. We all commented that the antelope was very tough and freezer-burnt for only one year in the freezer! He confessed after the meal that we just ate eleven-year-old antelope. Once, he served duck that was nine years old during the year 2000. The freezer package said 1990, but he changed the 0 to a 9 and now it read 1999.

Bullet

We had lots of dogs over the years, but one was very unique. His name was Bullet, and if there was any kind of real fur on any article of clothing, like a jacket, he would eat it. So we had to be very careful in the winter when we had parties, because that is when women would wear fur coats. We locked Bullet in the basement during parties so he could not get at the fur coats. During one winter party, Bullet somehow got out of the basement and found the coatroom. He settled in on a woman's unborn lamb's wool coat and ate a huge hole into the back of the coat. Someone could have thrown a football through the back of this coat when he was done. I was "Coat Boy" for the party, so I ran and quietly told Doc.

Doc said to me, "When she is ready to leave, hand me the coat folded in half. You open the front door and I will help her on with her coat, so her back will be turned to me."

It went like clockwork. Doc shook the husband's hand first, who went out to warm up the car. Doc then held her folded coat and asked her to turn around, to allow him to help her on with her coat. He put it on her and out she walked, with a big circle eaten out of the back of her coat.

Next day, she called up and said her coat was eaten at the party.

Doc said, "You looked good when you walked out of here last night, sounds like you might have a big moth problem over at your place."

She hung up the phone on him.

That same dog, Bullet, loved to ice fish. We would sit on crates and catch perch, dragging them onto the snow-covered ice. As soon as they were off the hook, Bullet would grab the fish in his mouth, with the perch sticking out of his mouth sideways like a cigar, and run around the ice hole in triumphant circles. The bigger the fish, the more excited he became.

One day, I had a big muskie on the line and I had to fight the fish for ten minutes. When I finally had him close to the hole, I made the mistake of standing up versus just trying to drag the big muskie onto the snow. When I stood up, it allowed the muskie to give a big tail kick and he exploded up out of the hole, creating slack in the line. As he flipped over to head back into the hole, he got off the hook. The muskie hit the hole with a big splash and quickly disappeared. Before I could react, Bullet dove into the ice hole to get the muskie. I quickly reached in after him without removing my winter glove or ski parka. I reached all around, with my entire arm and shoulder in the ice cold water, my neck and head pressed against the snow. I swished my arm around until the ice cold water made it numb and I would not have known if I felt the dog or not. I stood up in despair and planned to go tell my uncle, who was fishing in his ice shack twenty-five yards away. Suddenly, my uncle burst right through the side of his ice shack, blowing the plywood walls to smithereens! In his terror, he had not had time to open the door.

He had been daydreaming when Bullet popped up through his hole with a rush of choking and gasping, and my uncle thought it was some sort of lake monster! Uncle exploded out through the side of his ice shack, yelling and looking backward over his shoulder. I burst out laughing when I saw Bullet emerge from the ice hole, standing amid the splintered boards, shaking himself off and trotting toward me!

Deer Camp

We have a long-standing family tradition of heading up to our cabin in Northern Michigan for opening day of "Deer Camp." Every night, we play poker at our cabin, and the neighbors all come over. The usual cast of characters starts with me, Doc, and my Uncle Ted. That makes three Teds at the poker table, and all three Teds have a nickname.

Uncle Ted Black was known as "Blackie," my dad Ted was "Doc," and I was "TB." Mitch, "The Kielbasa King," was a large Polish immigrant who became head of engineering at Chrysler. Mitch's son, "Little Weiner," was there, plus three-fingered Randy, a local, and "Southside Willie" from the 19th Ward rounded out the table. The shenanigans around the table far outweighed the value of the pot on any given hand. One night, The Kielbasa King brought a loaded .45 to the table and announced, "Anybody cheat me, they gonna get it."

Mitch always lost badly and could not bluff, so he was convinced he was being cheated on a nightly basis. Blackie also could not bluff, and both these guys turned red-faced with excitement when they had a good hand. So everyone would fold because they both had such a transparent "tell." They would swear and we would roar with laughter. As Blackie and Mitch passed away, we would always "ante" for each of them. First Blackie died, and we honored him at the poker table with a second ante with each hand. Then a few years later, when Mitch passed away, we honored him with a third ante. So now a poker hand began with the dealer saying: "Everyone ante. Now ante again for Blackie. Now ante again for Mitch."

This prompted Doc's famous Yogi Berra line, "I can't afford to die, the ante would be too expensive for me!"

We once made the big mistake of inviting an outsider to play with us. He did not drink as much as we did, so he was out of sorts on the humor. When Southside Willie and I got into an old-fashioned "wrassle" and we tipped over backward out of our poker chairs, he got up and headed toward the door.

Doc yelled, "You're leaving?"

The guest stopped at the door, turned, and said, "I'm outta here, you guys are nuts." He was hesitating at the door, expecting Doc to plead with him to stay or apologize for our behavior. But instead, Doc reaches across the table and scrapes the guest's chip pile into his own pile, provoking more hysterical laughter from us. The guest turned and went out the door.

In the mornings at Deer Camp, we headed into the woods pre-dawn. Since we had stayed up late drinking and playing poker, we were hungover. If we had some toe and finger warmers, and it was not 0° degrees outside, we could doze off in our blind once we got comfortable. Southside Willy was in a ground blind, sitting on a chair, hidden in a brush pile. He slept right through the dawn. He woke up when he smelled something nasty. A big buck had walked into his blind, clearly intrigued by the hodgepodge of smells. I did not tell Willy that I had dabbed doe urine on his jacket, boots, shoes, and hat the night before, and he was too hungover to notice that the smell was coming from his clothes, as I had explained to him that I accidentally spilled a bottle of it where we hung all our clothes in the cabin. The buck had put his muzzle two inches from Willy's face and exhaled a big snort. Willy woke up, yelled in surprise and tipped over backward in his chair as the buck reeled and ran off.

Doc, Willy, and I would "sight" our rifles in the day before deer season. We would set up targets at one hundred fifty yards out, and test the scope on the guns. Willy and I were taping up the targets when, "Kaboom!" Doc fires a shot between us into the target board. Since we were only a foot apart, we jumped a foot into the air, scared to death. Then we heard Doc laughing, and we started cracking up at the audacity of his shot, right between our knees.

"I shot low just in case anything went wrong," he howled.

Hitchhiker

We decided to take a fishing trip to Montana, and we were going to carry backpacks and hike into streams and try fly fishing. We brought pepper spray because some Grizzlies can be aggressive. I put my pepper spray on the outside of my backpack in a mesh sleeve for a water bottle. We drove out to Colorado in our station wagon, with our backpacks just over the backseat.

In Nebraska, we picked up a hitchhiker, nice looking young guy, a college student heading west to do some backpacking. He got into the backseat and pulled his backpack onto the seat next to him.

After we exchanged pleasantries, Doc said, "Shove your backpack over the rear seat and give yourself some room there in the second seat."

The hitchhiker, Tod, said, "Sure" and he pushed his backpack over the seat on top of my backpack. My pepper spray was on the outside of my backpack, and his backpack accidentally hit the button on my pepper spray, and the spray nozzle faced toward the front of the car. In the flash of an instant, the car was filled with pepper spray.

We all yelled at the same time, Doc almost wrecked the car as he blindly pulled off the road and almost landed us in a ditch. All the windows were closed because it was raining outside. As soon as the car came to a rest, the three of us launched ourselves out of the car and immediately tumbled down a hill into a drainage ditch full of mud. We couldn't open our eyes, we couldn't breathe, and now we were covered in mud. We were moaning, groaning, thrashing around, and the stinging in the eyes and the burning throat was unbelievable. Then we noticed that the hitchhiker, Tod, was taking off into the woods. I could hear him crashing into trees, running blindly away from us. We had all been yelling and screaming, but now I stopped yelling and I heard him screaming, "Don't kill me, don't kill me!" as he ran blindly deeper into the woods.

In spite of our own agony, Doc and I suddenly burst into laughter as we simultaneously realized that poor Tod thought we sprayed him on purpose, that the back of the car was booby-trapped! Once we could function, over an hour later, we yelled for him, but he was probably ten miles away by then. We left his backpack in the ditch in case he ever came back for it. We wrote a note and put it on the backpack to explain how the freak accident had occurred.

Reel Foot Lake

We liked to take hunting trips, so we drove down to Reel Foot Lake in Tennessee in late November. The Tennessee Valley Authority had flooded thousands of acres of woodlands to build the Tennessee Valley Dam, a major hydroelectric dam for the area. In the process, they created Reel Foot Lake, one of the largest flood lakes in the world and a perfect hunting ground for ducks. The man-made lake was dotted with fallen trees that died from too much water, and that proved to be the perfect nesting ground for ducks. Hunters got up at 4:00 a.m. and headed out in small, thin, wooden rowboats with an outboard motor. The guides knew the swamp like the back of their hands. They were able to navigate their way around the stumps in the dead of night and take hunters out to a duck blind. The idea was to be in the duck blind before dawn, before the ducks started to fly.

So our guide rode us out in a little outboard that was extremely tippy, and we swore we were going to die as we saw tree trunks and stumps go whizzing by in the dark, less than a foot away from the side of the boat.

We got to our blind, which was a couple of wooden planks tied to poles sunk into the swamp, less than a foot above the ice cold water. The blind had camouflaged boards to hide behind, and was covered in cattails to hide the structure from the ducks. Picture a small baseball dugout on stilts that could hold four people, plus a guide and a dog. The idea was that the ducks started flying at dawn, and the guide called them in with his duck call, and told us when to jump up and shoot them. Then his dog would swim out and retrieve the dead ones.

So on this particular morning, our guide took us out to the blind. As we approached the blind, he realized he forgot the lunch cooler. We climbed into the blind in the pitch black, and the guide said he would go back to the dock and grab the cooler. He left the dog with us. Off he went, into the darkness, and we heard his engine grow fainter. Then we started to hear the engine sound grow stronger again. Strange, we said, he must be coming back to tell us something. The sound grew closer, but then pulled away again. He must have changed his mind, we speculated again. This pattern continued in the pitch black until it started to get light with the dawn.

As it got brighter, we now saw that the small boat was doing concentric circles, and the boat was getting ever closer to our blind with each circle. As the circle path of the boat grew closer to the blind, we saw that the guide was dead as a doornail. He had suffered a stroke or heart attack, and his hand was rigor mortis-clutched on the throttle and he was holding the throttle of the outboard at an angle that produced a perfect circle. That circle was moving closer and closer to the blind, and he was going maximum speed. In about two more circles, his outboard was going to blow right through our little duck blind, sending us all into the icy cold water of the swamp. In all of our heavy hunting gear, we were going to sink like rocks.

A quick debate ensued about what we should do.

"Let's shoot his hand off the throttle the next time he comes by," says Virgie.

"Bad idea" says Doc, "We will go to jail for manslaughter as they will think we killed him."

"Ok, then let's empty two of our shotguns, use them as pole extensions, and hang off the side of the blind. We will extend the kid with the help of the empty shotguns, and he can kick the guide's hand off the throttle as he comes by the next time."

"Great idea," everyone said except me, as I imagined falling into the freezing water or getting hit by the boat. But I hung out and waited for him. As he zoomed by, my out-stretched kick was about an inch short of reaching his hand as the boat flew by, and the next circle was going to bring him right into the blind at full speed.

We all got ready to jump for it, having shed our winter coats and boots to be able to climb out of the water. Here he came roaring in, right on target. We were all about to jump, when suddenly he ran out of gas twenty-five yards out and coasted right into the blind.

We tried to revive him with CPR, but he had been dead for a while. This was way before the day of cell phones, so since we were stuck until someone figured out we were missing. We tied the boat behind the blind and shot ducks all day, filling the boat and covering him up with ducks. The dog did a great job of retrieving the dead ducks.

It started to get dark and we had not eaten all day. We had no matches, it was getting cold, and we started thinking about having to spend the night in the duck blind because the guide boat had no gas. Finally, around nine p.m. we saw boat lights approaching. A search party brought us in, towing the dead guide and our ducks. The irony was that we had a very successful day of duck hunting without a guide calling in the ducks. The ducks came in anyway, and the dog did what he knew how to do without us giving him any commands.

Walloon Lake

Doc bought six hundred feet of undeveloped wooded lakefront property on a lake in northern Michigan. We started taking camping trips to the property as a family, with a pop-up trailer and tent. We dug a latrine, built a plank dock, got a canoe, and enjoyed the North Woods. There was an old dirt car trail along the lake that went through the property. The locals used what was now our property to have beer party bonfires. We blocked the road with logs and put up a "No Trespassing" sign.

One late afternoon, a pickup drove around the logs, through the woods, and right into our campsite.

Doc went up to the driver side window.

"This is my property, you are trespassing," Doc said.

The redneck said, "This is our fire pit area, we have been partying here for ten years."

"Not anymore," said Doc.

Redneck said, "We will be back tonight to retake our spot."

Doc said, "Hold on a minute."

He went into the pop-up trailer and came out with his .45 from Korea. "This will be waiting for you if you come back," he said, showing the pistol.

The pickup drove away. Wow, I was ten years old and just watched my dad turn into John Wayne.

I have always wondered if I would ever have the guts to do the same thing. The good news is that I don't own a pistol. What if the redneck had gotten out of the car and said, “So you gonna shoot me?” and then attacked Doc. What if the redneck also had a pistol with him? Lots of scenarios don’t play out like you want them to, but that one played out perfectly and they did not come back.

The consequences seem higher today, with a more litigious society. We all want to be John Wayne in the moment of righting a wrong. Once, I was in line at a burger drive-thru with my own three boys, and a car cut in front of me into the line. My oldest son said, “Dad, you gonna take that?”

It was a classic John Wayne test, with manhood at stake. Except I have no .45, no crowbar, and no martial arts. If I get outta my car and go up to his window, I’m 100% sure this guy will come out swinging; I saw his face as he cut into the line. He’s real angry already, looking for the altercation, waiting to explode. So I discuss the ramifications with my three sons. After I shared the downsides, they all came up with different reasons as to why I should not consider a John Wayne moment. It is exactly what I want them to conclude.

The sixteen-year-old said, “Too much career risk, even if you win and take the guy out.”

The twelve-year-old said, “You might lose and then we are all stuck here waiting for an ambulance, and who knows how long we would be stuck here.”

And the eight-year-old said, “We might not get the hamburgers we are about to order.”

None of them worried about me getting hurt, which was, of course, *my* biggest concern.

Airplane Ashes

Doc flew a small plane and had several friends who flew their own airplanes. Not jets, we're talking inexpensive entry-level planes like the Piper Cub and the Comanche. It was a two door, single-engine that held two adults and three small kids in the back, and not much room for luggage.

One of Doc's friends was trying to land in a storm one night in Boyne City, and he augured in and hit the side of Boyne Mountain and died. Another friend decided to pay tribute to his death by flying his own plane with the ash urn, and we would all be down on the lake in our boats, forming a circle, and the friend would fly over and drop the ashes into the boat circle. It was a tribute to the three things the dead guy loved: flying, boating, and Walloon Lake. The problem was that the friend up in the plane opened the small window of his plane as he was above us, and then he opened the lid of the ashes urn. The open window created a strong vacuum inside the plane, and as soon as he took the lid off the urn, the ashes all got sucked out of the urn and swirled around the cockpit. The ashes flew into his eyes and blinded him while he was trying to dump the urn out the window. Suddenly, his plane started spiraling down toward the circle of boats.

Doc started yelling, "He's coming in hot!" and there was a frantic rush to turn on boat engines and floor it away from the incoming plane.

The boats all dispersed just as the plane hit the water in an explosion of noise and plane parts, killing the pilot instantly on impact.

As we drove away in our own boat, Doc said, “I don’t think we should find a third pilot to fly over and try to dump both sets of ashes!”

Diving

Freddy Crouton and I were co-captains of the high school swim team. Since I goofed around on the high board after swim practice, the diving coach figured out that I could manage to do the five dives to get through a diving meet. I was not on the diving team, but if we had a diver out sick or the other team had only two divers in a meet, he would put me in the diving competition to pick up the 6th Place point. Sometimes we won a meet by only one point, so it could be worth it. If I was the sixth diver out of six, I knew I had the point, no matter what.

My buddy "Chiffon" Eddie, fellow diver, would give me $5 if I laid down the "mummy" off the high dive on my last dive during a summer outdoor meet. My last dive was always a reverse with a full twist off the high board. To do the mummy, I would purposely fail to rotate a full 360°, instead rotating 270° so my back was toward the judges. Then I would enter the water angled toward the judges, who were always sitting on the edge of the diving pool deck. As I angled in with my back to the judges, I sent a wall of water onto them and completely soaked them. My teammates would howl with laughter, as the judges would put up zeros for the dive, clearly not amused but unclear if they had been soaked on purpose or not. My skill level was shaky enough to leave uncertainty and avoid a DQ (disqualification) from the competition.

Doc would pull up outside the fence in his VW Bus and

open the sliding side door, and set up his own tailgate party with a bar and ice cooler. He'd sit and drink while he watched me dive. If he drank too much, he would lay on the horn after each of my dives, which was always very embarrassing. The judges and spectators would all turn their heads in wonderment at who could possibly be honking the car horn after each of my dives.

Doc was also known to bet other dads on the same swim team. "My kid will beat your kid in the fifty-yard free, five bucks!"

The other dads would stare at him in disbelief at his lack of "team" mentality.

High School Parties

My parents left us alone frequently in high school; what were they thinking? One night when they were out, my sister and I threw a big bash. This particular party got out of control, with way too many people showing up. We formed a fraternity in high school called the "Buffaloes," and when one of us (Keith, Rob, etc.) threw a party, we packed them in.

When my parents arrived home I was glad, since it had gotten out of hand. We got everyone out and we all went to bed around two a.m. At least, I *thought* we got everyone out.

At about three o'clock in the morning, I heard screams and then I heard Doc yell. My heart jumped out of my chest as I thought we were being robbed. I was frozen in bed with fear, straining to listen.

Then I heard Doc yell, "TB, get up here," so I knew there was no robber.

When I got up to their bedroom, there was a female high school classmate sitting on a chair in my parent's bedroom, holding her head in her hands.

I looked at my mom and dad. This girl had wandered around the house looking for a bathroom during the party, and she was so drunk that she mistook my parents' walk-in closet for a bathroom. She passed out behind a rack of clothes, and then woke up and tried to stumble out into the darkness. She walked out of their closet in the pitch black and when she ran into their bed, she pitched forward on top of my parents. All three screamed at once, as no one knew what was going on. She had no idea where she was. Of course, she vomited in the back of the closet before waking up, which was a lot of fun for me to clean up the next day.

Whenever my sister and I had a big party, I would put out bowls of Friskies Meal, the dry dog food pellets that we fed to our three hunting dogs. Then I told everyone they were ground-up dried hamburger pellets from Wisconsin. Every bowl was empty by the end of the night, and I never had to go buy pretzels. I didn't think anyone ever got worms or anything, and they actually went pretty well with beer, since they were crunchy and salty. Doc said, "Stop feeding all your drunk friends, you're running me out of dog food."

At another party at our house in the late fall, the cops came in and busted up the fun. High school kids went flying out the back doors as the cops came in the front door. It was pitch black out, and the kids were running to hide in the woods. Only my sister and I knew that we threw all the dog doo from three dogs down the steep hill behind the house, as well as all the leaves we raked. This created a semi-mulch of dead leaves and old dog doo on a steep incline. As the kids ran across the back yard, they did not see the hill in the darkness. They started tumbling down the hill, and when they stopped tumbling at the bottom, they had dog doo smeared all over them and rotten leaves stuck to the dog doo. They looked like a leafy dog doo version of The

Scarecrow from *The Wizard of Oz.* It was hysterical, but a bad ending for several high schoolers, who had to walk into their parents' house, covered in leaves and dog doo and trying to explain why.

In high school, Doc and I loved to compete against anybody in anything and bet $5 on the outcome. Golf, tennis, wrestling, pull-ups, foot races, pool, ping-pong, fishing, dove-shooting, you name it, if there was a way to bet someone, we created a competition. One night, our family was invited to the Bents' house for dinner. After dinner, we went down to the basement for a Ping Pong match: Doc and me against Bob Sr. and Bob Jr., who was my age. Doc and I beat them handily and so we decided to split up the teams to create a fair match and get a bet. Now it was Bob Jr. (a/k/a 12-Pack Bob) and me against Doc and Mr. Bent. Mr. Bent is 6'4", 250 lbs., and played football. Doc is 6'1", 225 lbs. Both have been drinking. There was not a lot of room on either side of the Ping Pong table; it was very tight quarters in this seventies-era rec room with the classic cheap wood paneling. Bob Jr. and I won the first game, and now the dads picked up the intensity, since they were losing the second game. Doc lunged for a shot, tripped over Mr. Bent's foot, and barreled into the side wall of the rec room. He happened to hit between the 2x4's behind the paneling and he blew through the plywood amid a huge crashing noise of splintering boards. He crashed through into the unfinished laundry room, where the cat litter box sat next to the furnace. He hit the furnace at full speed, which knocked him down into a seated position into the cat litter box. When he stood up, all the cat turds were dangling from the seat of his wool pants! We couldn't stop laughing, especially when Doc's first words were, "Cheap construction!"

Doc in High School

Doc was in high school when Hitler started invading Europe. There was a great concern that Hitler would eventually invade America if the United States did not enter the war. He and his friends decided it would be hysterical if they created a Nazi flag and hoisted it over the town hall one night, so the town would wake up and assume the Germans had taken over during the night. So it took them a month to cut and sew the flag, and then one night, they brought down the American flag flying over city hall and put up the Nazi flag. The next day, half the town was in a panic and the other half was in an uproar. They were caught when one in the group told his parents. The FBI came to town to interrogate them to ensure that it was simply a high school prank in bad taste, versus backing by some pro-Nazi sympathizers.

The Otter

The Cincinnati Zoo was hosting a black tie fundraiser, and they were bringing in the New York City Opera (with their famous Austrian Director) to perform in a big tent set up in the middle of the zoo. The event had been hyped for over a year, and hundreds were going, so Doc agreed to drive down from Middletown and attend.

Halfway through the opera, he was pretty bored, as opera was not exactly his thing. He quietly got up and slipped out through the seats, and everyone assumed he needed to go to the bathroom. He decided to walk around the zoo at 10:00 p.m. and see which animals were sleeping or not (diurnal versus nocturnal).

He came across the otter pen and they were all sound asleep. Their cage was set up with running water slides, and he wondered, if he woke up the otters, would they start playing on the water slides at night? A big otter was asleep with his back against the cage, curled up in a ball. Doc decided to poke him with his finger to see if he could wake him up. He poked him with his index finger. The otter reeled around as fast as lightning and bit his finger before Doc knew what happened. The sharp teeth ripped a gash in his finger that he knew needed stitches. He had a white handkerchief, and tightly wrapped it around his blood-soaked finger.

He walked back to rejoin his group, but there was no

admittance since the program was almost over. So he walked around the back and saw that he could enter through the back of the tent. He slipped into the back of the tent and realized that he was now backstage, behind the opera performers and not on the audience side. It was pretty dark, so he sneaked up behind one of the stage props that create the scenery on stage. There was a hole the size of a Dixie cup for him to look through, so he watched for a while through his private peephole. He was looking through the opera out at the audience. The performance was soon over, and he was still on stage behind the props. A standing ovation occurred, the lights went up, and he watched the opera stars walk past him backstage to their makeshift dressing rooms. The director of the opera walked past just as Doc stepped out. The Director assumed he was a big donor, or why else would he be backstage? He came up to Doc to shake hands, beaming from his performance. He wanted to bask in the glow of accolades, and he reached out to Doc with both hands, Euro style. Then he saw Doc holding a bloody handkerchief over his finger.

"Vat happened to zee hand?" asked the Austrian Opera Director.

"The otter bit it," Doc replied.

"Zee otter in zee zoo?" he asked.

"Yes," Doc replied, "zee otter in zee zoo."

"Zee otter is loose?" asked the famous Director.

"No, not loose, in his cage," Doc answered.

"Vhat ver you doing in zee otter cage?" asked the director.

Doc saw he was baffled. "Zee otter was asleep and I poked it through zee bars to wake it up," Doc replied.

"Zo you left your seat during zee performance?"

Now Doc saw where he was coming from; the man's face was conveying sadness and dismay that Doc may not have liked the performance.

"No, no, zee performance was superb, but I needed to stretch zee legs. Zee opera was fantastic!"

"Ahh, zank you so much, I am glad you liked it! We leave a little beet of ourselves in Zinzinatti."

And Doc replied, holding up his finger, "And me too, I leave a little beet of myself in Zinzinatti," and they both roar with laughter.

Doc's dinner table friends were in disbelief that Doc had a one-on-one conversation with the Director of the New York City Opera, one of the most famous people in the world at the time.

Doc's 81st Birthday

We decide to honor Doc's 81st birthday with a song, just like we did for his 60th. My sisters and I wrote the lyrics, sung to the tune of *The Beverly Hillbillies* theme song from the television show in the late sixties:

"COME LISTEN TO THE STORY 'BOUT A
MAN NAMED TED"

Come listen to the story 'bout a man named Ted,
Glenn Jackson said, "He's got brains in that egghead!"
"Go to Lake Forest and get yourself a copper roof,"
But he said, "I prefer cow manure under the hoof."
    Middletown, that is.
    Few swimming pools, no movie stars.

Then he went to Korea where he shot geese and quail,
At med school and dental school he raised a little "heyll."
He got his DDS and went back to Middletown,
Where he said, "Guess it's time now for me to settle down."
    Rosedale, that is.
    Gaker family beside, Verity family behind.

Well the first thing you know he found Nancy for a spouse.
They had three kids after building them a house.
He won some at golf, and some at tennis too,
But at trap and skeet he won 'bout 92.
    Trophies, that is.
    Big ones.
    Little gold hunter on top.

Now Ted liked to fish, and he liked to sail too,
He saw some land in Michigan on pretty Lake Walloon.
He said, "I'll buy a bunch of that and do some camping now,
And if its value rises I can buy an extra cow."
    Genius, that was.
    Goldmine.

Well Ted is quite the hunter and shot mountain goat and bear,
In search of great adventure he goes traveling everywhere.
On African safari he faced down a charging lion,
Then sewed up a guy he found leopard-mauled and dyin'.
    Hero, he was.
    Hemingway style.

Now, Doc can do a lot of things although he'd never boast;
He flew his own plane and he's strong from sinking post.
He skied the black diamonds and he scuba-dived too,
And he doesn't lose at shooting pool unless he's had a few.
    Cocktails, that is.
    Generation thing.
Well the Highlander went over when his shoes slipped off the deck,
Roundups were a bust when he says, "cows can go to heck."
The logs from Boyne Mountain sure do make a nice fire,
Raising rheas sounds easy, what could that require?
    Chaos, sometimes.
    Lots of fun though.

How 'bout those family sailing trips to islands in the south,
Or the hunting and fishing trips for deer, elk, and trout.
He only met one man for whom he didn't give a hoot,
We'll always remember the yellow banana boots.
    Friendly, he is.
    Quite a character.

Well Ted is quite the nature guy; he knows 'bout every bird;
Once he raised some falcons, and he tried a rhea herd.
He knows the stars, the trees, and every fish and every beast,
And if you're lost in any woods, he knows which way is east.
    Born with it, he was.
    We kids weren't.

Then he married Marilyn, and what a pair they make;
They're a winning team at bridge and she pulls him from the lake.
She's also an artist, and he of course is not,
But we're just thrilled at this relationship they've got.
    Romance and everything.

We were all going to celebrate his big 8-0,
But then TB said, "Doc, let's hunt in Mexico!"
Well, getting Doc home from there was no mean feat,
With a broken hip and his bottom stuck to a plastic cushion seat.
    Expensive, that was.
    We're talking Medjet prices.

Then Doc was in Chicago in some real intensive care,
But he gave a shout for Mol to come and bust him out of there.
Therapy and doctor visits gave him quite a year,
So we had to delay the time we'd finally get here.
    Party time, now.
    Belize style.

Now, Doc will tell a tale until we're rolling on the floor;
He's had some good adventures and he'll have a whole lot more.
He's Renaissance Ted and he's sure a lot of fun,
So we proudly salute him on his big 81.
    Birthday, that is.
    Have a good one, Doc.

The End.

Doc with sister Marty

The farm house,
Martin Meadows

Doc with his dad, big duck day

Doc with pet hawk

Doc loves cats

Doc and Ted Jr. at deer camp

Ringo gets air

NATURAL BORN Killer

NATURAL BORN Dead - Eye

NATURAL BORN Horseman

NATURAL BORN Fighter

Author Ted Martin, Jr. with sisters Jill and Molly, dog Bullet, and trophy-winning steer "Blackie"

Doc and grandsons

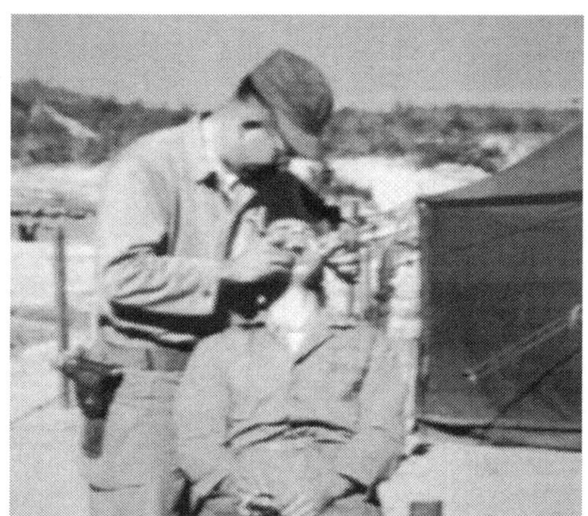

Doc fixes teeth in Korea

Doc is the small boy at the harvest

Doc gets his deer

Nick, Oak, Nance and Ted Martin, Jr.

Doc catches breakfast